PROFOUND BLESSINGS

By

CATHERINE CAPRA-LEAF

ISBN-10: 1475225369
ISBN-13: 978-1475225365

PROFOUND BLESSINGS

The spirit of the heart.

It leads us to places that we may not expect to go,

But hold on tight to the sails,

For the ride is rich and full of grace

This book is dedicated to all of those who have walked this profound journey with my children and me. Your strength, love and dedication to a man who walked this earth, loved his family and celebrated all of you, is why this book was written. It is my deep hope that you feel blessed by our family's journey, and that it embraced your spirit.

To those of you who have witnessed the spiritual journey to heaven of loved ones, may God bless you, and may you hold close to your heart the profound blessings that carried you through your own personal journey.

My deepest gratitude goes to the staff at the Mayo Clinic in Rochester, Minnesota, who each day lit a candle of courage for us. They were champions for our cause, and fought a daily battle bravely and vigilantly for Mike. Their daily compassionate care never wavered, and is something I will keep in my heart forever.

Healing Compassion…a most profound blessing.

TABLE OF CONTENTS

For my children, Jennifer, Kimberly and Heather…
You lead me to my rainbow everyday…

1 THE CANVAS FOR THE DAY

My favorite secret place. I felt a calling to return here. It was a place that I found one day after the monster came, when I needed to remove my heart from all of its surroundings, to release it, let it be free, where it didn't have to dwell in the house of the monster, if only for a day.

As I stood overlooking the cliff, I couldn't help but remember *the dream*; the chronic dream of falling off a cliff, a cliff that haunted my dreams every night. When sleep would finally come, it was interrupted with the event. I was falling, helpless, and unable to control it. I stood close near the edge and looked down. Standing there, I finally felt the ability to confront the enormous fear that took the shape of jagged rocks and a steep cliff. It was the dream of a woman who was fighting hard to survive. To put it on canvas that day felt cathartic and healing. I would need all the energy that this magical place had to give for such a brave task.

The beautiful North Shore of Lake Superior. I came here today because I needed a place far away from the world that was familiar. The chill of the air here is direct, beautiful. The late October wind was leaving its ominous message that winter was imminent, and the icy energy of change was reflected in the lake's spirit. Its shores were spattered with ebony boulders, and the waves crashed hard onto them, as if it were a warning of transformation. The seasons were changing, and the world here was turning an indifferent cheek, as the summer winds had shifted. The water was chilling, preparing for its annual petrifaction of winter's grandest of ice sculptures and snow-covered earth.

The beauty of the waters is so intense and severe, yet so beautiful and captivating, that it takes my breath away. It is powerful, but has a sense of tenderness. I feel it calling those who need its strength. It is a place of peace. Spiritual waters so grand, they needed to have a shoreline of jagged cliffs and eclectic clusters of beautiful ebony boulders to frame its magic. It was as if God just shook a saltshaker and it all landed where it needed it to be. It's why I returned here. *My desperate longing to know where to land.*

The sunrise had made its voyage across the sky earlier in the day, leaving crimson brush strokes in its wake. The beauty of the canvas changed as the day did. A large ship carrying taconite was crawling slowly against the backdrop of the horizon; its monotone horn indicated its arrival into port. A slow moving cadence, that reminded me of a circus elephant, strong and slow, yet steadfast in its task. There were seagulls dotting the skies, and the smell of pine, and pungent earth had awakened my senses. It was God's place. It was a place of enormous spirit, a place where prayers and thoughts were given over to the powers of the universe, a direct path to God. And this place of enormous energy seemed to understand its own power and welcomed those who came to seek answers.

And so this morning I took a long walk up a hillside path that led me to an open clearing that overlooked a beautiful cliff. I could hear the strong waves crashing against the rocks below. Standing there, gave me a feeling of comfort as I wrapped myself in its strength.

I looked for a place to rest and found it on a boulder. I climbed up on it, and sitting on it was surprisingly comfortable. It was as if it was meant to be sat upon. I really didn't know what to do, except to breathe. I am ready with my canvas and brushes to capture it all… but in this moment; my hands are unable to move. The journey up here was mine, fulfilling a need to be alone. But my heart did not want to be alone. There was a wave of sadness that I did not expect. The moment had become too big emotionally to be here alone. My thoughts raced and ran rampant as to whom I wanted here with me. But I didn't have the bravery to answer that for myself; yet.

It was a worn path that led me here, and from the beaten down earth and shoe prints, it was apparent that it had brought many up to the cliffs. But I was unprepared for who else was about to climb the path today. As I looked at the skies and took in the energy, I began to hear slow methodical footsteps. I saw a shadowed figure walking into the grassy clearing. The cadence in his stride had not changed and he was using a cane. He was a tall man, statuesque, and yet frail. His hands and arms would shake and twitch, but he seemed comfortable with it and it did not make him waver.

He walked over to the cliff, unaware of my presence. He stood lost in his thoughts, staring at the water as if he had found an old friend. He took out a small black book and held it in his hands and placed it over his heart. My presence here felt invasive and I felt frozen, trying not to move or make a sound. He finally turned away from the hill and our eyes met. His handsome brown eyes immediately intrigued me. He smiled at me and his presence felt warm. I was happy to have a cliff-side companion. He wore a large green jacket made for this kind of weather, but it had seen better days. He must

4

have been a local; familiar with this place, and my guess is that it may have been his special place too. He walked over to me with a smile on his face. "Well, well," he said, "to whom do I have the honor to share the heavens with today?"

I smiled. "Someone who needed to find the heavens today," I replied.

For some reason it felt important not to tell him who I was. He smiled and seemed to understand, and looked away from me to the water and took in a deep, breath. He chose not to share his name either. This was the first moment of unsaid boundaries that we shared, and he became very still as his eyes looked over the cliff, and the blue canvas of water. His thoughts were in deep places, and I could see the emotion in his eyes. I instantly knew that his was a journey of the heart, and it had led him here. After a few moments he looked over at me. "You're sittin' on a piece of magic," he said.

I jumped up. "Oh please, sit down, is this your place to sit?" I asked. "Would you like to rest a bit?"

He stopped for a moment then spoke with softness in his voice that I didn't expect, with the grace of an angel. "No," he said. "God has made this your place to sit today dear" and he pointed to another place where he would sit to rest.

It was such a beautiful thing to say, I thought to myself. I felt tears well up in my eyes listening to the kindness of his words. Moments of subtle kindness always made me tear up in those days. Were my eyes as resonating as his? Did he see right through them? Did he notice right away that they were green, as I noticed his were brown? His face was full of character. A story baked into his soul. All I knew for sure was that this moment in time was to be spent with a stranger; a man who had climbed up a hill and landed next to me. He knew God's plan for the boulder I was sitting on today. It was the most serendipitous moment that I had ever felt.

And so, a day that I planned for solitude became a day I shared with a new friend, just when I'd thought that the loneliness had become unbearable. I shared a thermos full of coffee and a head full of thoughts with him. He seemed as comforted as I did to have company. I wondered what his calling was today. After talking, we sat in comfortable silence together, neither of us quite ready for more conversation.

Quietly, a little baby squirrel had shown up from behind a tree. We both smiled and welcomed the newcomer. He put his frail and shaking hand into his pocket and pulled out a handful of field corn for his little friend. He worked hard to steady his hand as he opened it. Ever so slowly, he lowered his shaking body to the ground, and placed the corn on the grass. A smile beamed across his face and his gaze was transfixed. It was a chance to be purposeful again, to feed his little friend. He looked over at me with a twinkle in his eye. "Say hello to Sadie," he said, still smiling.

I looked at the little creature that had not moved; frozen and trying to trust us; or perhaps, trying to trust me. The little creature had a name. My new friend was a frequent flier to the cliff, I thought to myself. He and Sadie had obviously shared other moments. Fascinated, I became increasingly intrigued by him. My curiosity was overwhelming as I tried to guess the reason for his journey here today. Sadie bravely inched her way to the field corn. And I slowly found the courage to trust myself, to be a friend to the old man with intriguing brown eyes.

As his attention focused on his little friend, he began to unfold bits and pieces of the story that brought him here. We were two people who met by chance on a cliff side retreat. Two people who understood the enormity of cliffs and the importance of slaying the dragons.

When he was sure that Sadie had enough food, he slowly put the rest of the corn back into his pocket. He sat back on his boulder for the day, and looked out over the cliff. He drew back and looked at me and smiled. "It's a beautiful day for a visit, isn't it?" he asked.

I knew he wasn't talking about our visit; he was talking about visiting someone in heaven, just as I was.

And for the next few hours I was given the privilege to hear about Kathryn. She was the love of his life. She was a woman of strength and love for the ages. I was honored that he was sharing her name with me, though he still hadn't share his. I would play this game. It gave both of us anonymity for our pilgrimages.

They had met when he returned from the war, the war where he fought his dragons. He stopped short of telling me of the events that unfolded so long ago, in a land so far away. Men his age rarely spoke of these things. I had learned this from my father, whose cabinet of medals and military decorations told the story all too well. My new friend was once a brave young soldier, handsome and strong, before the years had taken their toll.

They met when he returned from the war. She was the most beautiful woman he had ever met. His eyes were transfixed on the memory of her beauty. And as his story unfolded, she must have been transfixed too, her love for the ages. Their paths had gone in many different directions. They came in and out of each other's lives through hardship and circumstance. But when they found refuge in each other, they would only share moments of tenderness and love. Theirs was a love story that transcended both time and place. It was as if the world would spin and go on, but their time together was frozen, captured in each other's hearts, in deep shadowed areas were no one was aware.

I had understood this story. This love.

As he told me the story of his love, I felt tears welling up in my eyes again, but I kept them hidden from him. I didn't want him to stop. He was stuck here in this old body, riddled with infirmity of his age. As he spoke of her and their love, there was a sense of excitement for him as if he knew that they would be together again soon, finally. And so I was honored with the story of Kathryn. She was his intoxicating liqueur that made his heart skip a beat, and made him lose his breath, even now as he spoke of her. Somewhere in the story he stopped cold. His focus turned to me.

"And so you have lost love, my dear?" My head darted away as I didn't see this coming. I heard the waters crashing hard against the boulders down below. The sound was diversionary; I was caught off balance, and not ready to answer. The waves of sadness were almost too much to bear today. But his smile was reassuring, and he walked over to me with his trembling old frame, sat down and grabbed my hand. I felt his uncontrollable shake, but he had a firm, strong hold on me nonetheless. I could barely breathe much less speak of it all. "Yes," I said, "he was an incredible man who loved me, and we shared a life". "I came here to find peace with his death, to find peace with my life".

He was silent and looked to the heavens for a moment and then looked back at me. His beautiful brown eyes smiled into mine, he put his hand on my shoulder and understood the importance of my painful answer, my quest to overcome the cliffs.

He whispered softly, "You have come to the right place," His mystical deep brown eyes peered soulfully into mine. "You have lost love, but you are also preparing your heart to weave a golden tapestry aren't you?"

My body went cold and my thoughts were frozen. He smiled. "You are very brave," he said. "It is a beautiful thing to embrace love." He pulled out the old leather book from his pocket and chose his words carefully. And with a deep sigh he said, "These are my precious memories of Kathryn. Although our lives were full of passions and other loves, we knew that ours was spun with God's golden thread. It is a beautiful gift from the heavens to be blessed with such a love." He then placed the black book in my hand.

"My stories of her keep her alive for me, and when I see her in my dreams I know it is time to come here, a place that transcends all love. The mystical waters here are heavenly. You must find a way to keep love close to you, tangible, and keep your memories warm. Find a way my dear, find a way to leave this place today and paint your canvas; your passion, your love, your story."

I will never forget this wonderful man. He gave me the sword I needed to slay the dragon; to understand the importance of keeping it all etched in my mind, so it could be remembered and stay warm. And it was with his words that I felt the calling to write the story of my heart. This is my story, of my love and my loss, and my search to weave the golden threads of it all into the life that I have ahead of me.

I will never forget my encounter at the North Shore; my serendipitous encounter with a man, who walked up the hillside in an old and frail frame, to make his love tangible, and teaching me to do the same. The old worn black book was all he had left in this world. But it was all he needed, and it kept him walking up hillsides to be with her. Meeting this old man on a cliff side journey was extraordinary. He was a brave and beautiful man, who taught me to capture my memories and keep them warm.

A serendipitous encounter… A most profound blessing

2 DESPERADOS

The Eagles. The car radio was playing one of my favorite songs by one on my favorite bands. Singing of a desperado needing to come to his senses: he was out riding fences too long! Kari turned it up and looked at me with a smile. She was a wonderful friend who was my life support now. She was someone who kept me as brave as I possibly could be, for my family and my dying husband. We were driving back to the hospital. It would be the first of many road trips in the year to come. A safe haven in a car, when the rest of the world could be at a distance and intimate conversations between friends had no boundaries.

"How are you doing? Kari said as she found a small grin, trying not to look concerned.

My leg was on the dashboard trying to make peace with the pain in my back. I just looked at her and smiled, then opened the window and started to sing along with the Eagles. As I looked out the window, I breathed in the cool spring air. It was as if it was desperately trying to awaken me and keep me in the game.

"Desperados" was the perfect song for the moment. "Why don't you come to you senses?" A good question, I hadn't been able to come to my senses for such a long time. The journey in the last year was like an endless rollercoaster. The twists and turns in the path gave me whiplash and I was holding on for dear life with a white knuckled grip.

My life as I knew it had disappeared.

On what seemed a lifetime ago on a warm summer day, I heard the front door open. The door opened as it did everyday at 6:05, and I was greeted with a smile, a kiss, and if it was Wednesday, my favorite chocolate from a street vendor downtown. But this day, his warm and kind demeanor was marked with an unusual paleness, and the twinkle that was in his steel blue eyes that always greeted me had been dimmed.

"What's up Mike?" I said as my thoughts turn to concern. I instinctively knew it was important. Recent headaches and memory loss had landed him in the doctor's office a week earlier.

"The doctor called me today and said the MRI showed I had a small stroke" he said with an ominous tone to his voice that I had never heard before. He sat on the couch and stared out the window with his briefcase still in his hand. He was a 52-year-old man who was physically fit, an exceptional athlete, and full of life. A lover of all sports, he excelled at the game of golf and played as often as he could. He was man who was spiritually centered and had simple values. No one could have predicted the walk he was about to take. What just happened? It was the first of many moments of this journey that I felt shards of glass breaking all around me. It marked the end of the last normal moment of our lives.

He was a man who was strong, healthy, and in a blink of an eye was dealt a new hand. As he stared out the window on that summer day, dressed in his corporate "importance" with his Armani tie hiked up over his shoulder, I knew we were both naked, balancing on a fencepost in a world that had shifted. More like a seismic event under the earth's surface.

The next several months were marked with events spiraling out of control. He was hospitalized many times with unexplainable seizures and strokes, that later was diagnosed as a rare autoimmune disease called Antiphospholipid Syndrome which caused a swelling of the blood vessels in his brain. His strokes had affected his speech, sight, and cognitive abilities. My job became "dignity patrol". Job layoffs, declining health, physical therapy, tests, and doctor's visits battered our days. Our entire life as we knew it had been put on the back burner, and nothing else mattered.

During one of his last hospital stays near our home, I felt the mood shift. The doctors became quiet and their demeanor had changed, as concern blanketed their faces. Difficult and painful tests came up with nothing, as his body started wasting away. There were no answers for any of it. *They were lost and I knew it,* and none of them could pull a rabbit out of a hat. But I could… I had to. I knew there were more rabbits, more hats. My own body had met the cancer monster in the last couple of years. Looking back, I now know that scary moment in my life was preparing me for this path. It taught me to reach deep. I learned through that experience the art of being an assertive health care recipient. Its street name was "a bitch". When dealing with the monster of illness and death, there were times when being a bitch became the only playing card I had left, the only hat. I spent hours memorizing medical records and health history. I armed myself with information that made me a warrior in a conference room filled with white coats, insisting that no stone be left unturned.

In the next several months, the important things of this world changed quickly. And just as quickly, I put on my Super Woman suit and became of woman of power and strength. To save the world, or "our" world, and eradicate the evil nemesis that had landed on our doorstep. The last rabbit I could muster up had brought us here, to the Mayo Clinic. And so on a warm sunny day in March, we arrived here with hope in our hearts. The plan was to come as an outpatient, but soon after we arrived, he was admitted immediately with unexplainable pain in his abdomen that brought us rushing through the doors of the ER.

The doctors went to work. In the next couple of weeks, the finest minds put on their hardhats and beat away at his sickness with state of the art treatments, tests, and therapy. Cancer was always a major suspect, but it had not been supported in any test results. Their unique comprehensive approach to medicine was organized into different teams of specialized doctors, each throwing their best cards on the table. Teams of Cardiologists, Internists, Neurologists, Oncologists, "Rabbit"ologists…all warriors in their own right, trying to find the lost piece of the puzzle that might keep him in the game. In the days to come, our family would understand the importance of finding a missing puzzle piece. But the charge continued on in this place, this medical think tank. Doctors from all over the country ended up at his bedside with swarms of medical students. Batteries of new cutting edge tests were performed; and we waited.

Then one quiet afternoon, the head of oncology walked into the room with a file full of test results. I looked at it, and I looked at him, and tried to eek out a polite smile. We took a walk down the hall and he patiently and compassionately tried to explain the unexplainable. None of the tests had been positive for cancer, there were no answers as to what was ravaging in his body. It should have been a relief to know that cancer had been for all intents and purposes ruled out, but my exhausted head desperately needed an answer. He took my hand and kindly explained that oncology would now take a back seat, but promised other doctors would take up the charge and they would continue to fight hard to come up with answers…to find one more rabbit.

But in the end, *we had run out of rabbits.* After a last resort exploratory diagnostic surgery, the monster had been unveiled, and doctors recoiled in disbelief and sadness. The nemesis was finally given a name of an ugly illusive cancer that had imploded in his body. An unexplainable fluid had encapsulated inside of him, and enveloped his organs. It had hidden it all! At that moment it became clear. I knew then that God wanted him more than we needed him, and he was not be meant to be saved. Sometimes you just know things.

I had taken off my Super Woman suit, and never put it on again.

So many months ago, on that warm summer day, in a sad and life defining moment, I watched this wonderful man, my husband, stare out the window lost in the abyss of fear. A beautiful man, who had been blindsided, and had no idea of what he was about to endure, a man who didn't deserve this path. My heart instinctively knew that the winds of change would be unforgiving…and they were. All of which had ended me up here, driving in a car with a dear friend at my side, an empty hat, and a cool splashing of fresh air on my face…to keep me in the game.

As Kari listened to me sing with the wind in my face, she smiled and rolled her eyes at me, and looked the other direction. Concern and fear entered her thoughts, and she didn't want me to see it in her face. She instead concentrated on the road signs.

The highway sign declared: **St. Mary's Hospital - 2 Miles Ahead**. It was the only place that captured hope for the moment, and it was the only place that had the power to take it away.

"And here we are!" Kari proclaimed.

"Yes, here we are, the Temple of Doom" I said, void of any emotion. The building itself was beautiful, made of the finest granite and marble. It was indeed a temple. In the evening, it was lit up as if it were a beacon in the night. The history of the Mayo Brothers was rich, and the hospital that was built in their name was to cure the sick, research diseases and offer hope. But for us, this had been a week of bad news that extinguished all hope for recovery. His body was giving in. It was a week of incredible change, sadness, and direction for my life. It was when my prayers shifted, and my thoughts were now in the direction of impending change. And even though we lovingly called this place "The Temple of Doom," my heart will always be grateful for the many care providers who worked around the clock to keep him in the fight.

As the music played of a sad desperado, I was happy to be in a car with my friend Kari, who kept a clear head and processed the latest news with me. She was willing to talk about "the latest horrible event of the day" as long as I needed to, and she seemed to know when to be silent. A good friend since childhood, and though we have lived very different lives in different areas of the country, our friendship has always been gold. Who would have thought that friendship would land here? *When does a friend morph into a lifesaver?* When I called her with the news that the ominous monster would take its shape as an unforgiving cancer, Kari got on a flight as fast as she could and declared with resolve, "I'll stay as long as you need me." Her life went on hold. Her dance studio was scheduled with substitute teachers. Recital costumes went unordered, and we were left wondering every night if her mom was taking her meds. Nevertheless, none of it really mattered. I could see it in her eyes.

There are times when you feel wrapped in blessings. It changes you forever.

The day Kari arrived; she put her arms around all of my children. They knew she loved them. They shared conversations that I was not a part of. They were no longer children, but were grieving young women trying to be brave.

"I'm in charge of cell phones," Kari said, "and liquor, car keys, and crying daughters".

"Oh my God, she's Mary Poppins on crack... perfect!" I proclaimed.

They all laughed and hugged her, and they were happy to have her there with them. She took care of everything that I was unable to. Kari never wavered from her duties, and I know she understood the enormous help that she was to me. She cared for me like a wounded kitten, and helped me navigate through my darkest days. My new world that was changed by cancer and disease. It was the first time in my life that I felt as though I couldn't put one foot in front of the other. Laughter was our best medicine, and evenings were topped of with a glass of wine on the deck of the hotel.

We were Desperados.

So the journey of incredible sadness and change of focus started earlier this week, sitting in a large Temple of Doom conference room with grim faced doctors, as they rattled off what to expect for the "end ". The next few weeks would bring the most difficult moments for my family, who would walk the walk with me, and I with them.

Kari, Keeper of the Keys, opened the door to the hotel room.

"OK, Miss Desperado, here you are at your very own Hotel California. I smiled and thought to myself, finally a place to press the off button. It was dark and there was the presence of sleeping children. The TV was blaring and there were remnants of their dinner on the nightstands. There were cards, letters, and gift baskets from loving friends everywhere, loved ones who lifted us up every day and comforted us with their concern and prayers. It became important to continue my concert live and unplugged.

"OK," Kari said, "you need wine now, and I need you to have wine now!" She then smiled and put a glass of merlot in my hand.

"I thought Mary Poppins was in charge of spoonfuls of sugar?" and I continued to sing back at her, with my awesome singing voice.

Were we really here? Were our lives uprooted and changed forever? I didn't understand the change. I didn't understand this fear. I put on my softest flannel pants and Mike's tee shirt. It smelled of him. I crawled into my bed that I shared with my daughter, Kimberly. Jennifer and Heather were sleeping in the bed next to us. My thoughts turned to the incredible sadness I felt for them. As they lay sleeping, I wondered where their dreams were taking them tonight. I wished I could have crawled into their dreams and hugged them. Exhaustion had set in their weary heads. Amazingly, none of the little angels woke up from my rendition of the Eagles "unplugged" hit parade.

My Hotel California was every bit as cluttered with chaos as the minds of those who lay sleeping there. The *Bat Phone* was put on the charger and I tried to get comfortable in my bed. Suddenly, sleep became a frightening thought. The inability to be aware of anything during an unconscious state would mean that I was losing control of it. My head hit the pillow, but my eyes could not close.

Tomorrow would be another day, and I was afraid of what it would bring. And even then I could not close my eyes, but it was comforting to feel my children's presence around me. I turned over and looked at my cell phone: the *Bat Phone*. It was named for its super powers at the Temple of Doom. It was indeed a superhero's tool, ready to take on the emergency messages of the moment. It was a small but very powerful thing in my life. It was a vessel that connected me to all that was changing, sometimes moment-to-moment. In a time when I trusted nothing in my daily existence, it connected me with heartfelt concern and prayers from those I loved. At the same time, it also brought dire messages in monotone voices that brought news of serious medical updates. It was also the conduit that told loved ones news that would profoundly change their lives. It was a power of both good and evil, it became a trusted and scary companion.

I reached over, picked it up and set in on my pillow, as I anticipated the news that may arrive in the middle of the night like a lightning bolt. I looked at it curiously every night, and it was the last thing I saw. I stared at it as if it were a wild creature, daring it to ring before my eyelids collapsed like dungeon doors. Its silence comforted me like a worn soft blanket comforts a vulnerable child; for when it remained silent...my life was silent. It was a time to take a deep breath, and take in a quiet moment.

Grief and fear are powerful companions. I learned to understand the connection. They enabled me to do crazy things to survive the storm that crashed through my mind. My *crazy* was sleeping with a red phone clenched in my fist, as it was the only way I could find peace.

I rolled over and looked at Kim who was sharing my bed. Her tear-stained eyes were closed and she was breathing slowly and peacefully as she had as a small child. My grown up daughter looked very childlike sleeping next to me, and I felt comforted by it. I leaned over and kissed her cheek, and noticed something clenched in her hand as well. It seems that someone else knew the significance of a *Bat Phone's* silence, when there was

nothing left…but an empty hat.

A Bat Phone's Silence… A most profound blessing.

3 TIME IN A BOTTLE

The sun had come up beautifully this morning. Spring was feeling its way into the world. I sat on a bench in an area of the hospital that was meant for reflection. The warm morning sun felt so good against my face; a time to brush off yesterday's events and prepare for the unknown events that would come this day. The children had all gone home to make arrangements in their own lives so they could return to stay here as long as they needed to. In a few hours they would be returning, to wait out the monster, all landing together to walk through the journey. We would wait together; they were my "core". Pain and heartache were the ties that bound us together, so too were strength and bravery. It was an awakening for us. We felt the tide of change. Our roles were shifting right before our eyes. *There is such strength in family when we are together*, I thought to myself. His three beautiful daughters, here to be a champion for his cause, fight for his dignity, and learn to draw on their character and be what their father would have wanted them to be.

"Dad, Get up! It's morning!" She shouted.

He rolled over in bed and was face to face with a little blue- eyed girl in pigtails, reindeer feet pajamas, and a favorite worn blanket in her hand.

He smiled. "Why?" he asked.

She looked irritated and started pulling at his arm. "Because Dad, it's Christmas! He came! We have to open presents! C'mon!"

He winked at me with a smile. "Who came?" he asked.

She looked at him with the most perplexed look and framed his face with her little four-year-old hands, as if she needed to explain it all to him so he could understand. Her eyes looked deeply into his. "Dad, Santa comes on Christmas Eve because of Jesus, remember? Didn't you hear the reindeer on the roof last night? They were very loud! Now get up, hurry! It's time to open presents!"

I rolled over in bed. "Good thing you got straightened out on that one, honey" I said. "I'll make the coffee." I rolled over and looked at the alarm clock that was flashing 4:55. We got out of bed and smiled at each other. Another warm Christmas morning was about to unfold and I remember thinking of our blessings. I walked into the living room and Miss Jennifer had her younger sisters, all in matching pigtails and reindeer pajamas, placed on the couch like little Babushka dolls. And so that Christmas, like so many others to follow, was filled with joy and happiness, and the innocent love of little girls who grew to become beautiful women. Christmas presents changed through the years from baby dolls and tea sets to their favorite jeans, CDs and video games. A family Christmas wrapped in love.

Three little Babushka girls sitting on a couch. They had learned through the years to support and comfort each other, and understood the love of their father. He was a man who guided them through their childhood with kindness, steadfast values, and loved them unconditionally. A man who was strong, and taught them early in life the value of character, work ethic, trust and humor.

The most important gifts they would ever receive, were not found under the Christmas tree.

"Hey mom," I felt Jennifer's warm arm wrap around my neck behind me. I was so glad she and her sisters were all finally going to be together again today. After the news that their dad's passing was imminent, she got back on a plane, this time with her boyfriend Micah. She was now living in California and they returned on a flight as fast as they could. She was so tired and sad, but felt the need to step up. She was the oldest daughter, who always felt the need to care for us, and felt the shifting rolls in family members. It was her need to place the Babushka dolls on the couch in the right order.

"I've been looking for you mother", she said as she hung onto my neck.

"Are you OK?" she asked.

I hugged her back and kissed her forehead.

She laughed and said..."I know, it sucks...every little bit of it sucks."

We both stared at the beautiful gardens with thoughts that neither one of us were ready to share.

"Where is Micah, Sweetie?" I asked as she put a cup of coffee in my hand.

"He's back at the room."

He was a beautiful soul, and I am so glad they found each other. It felt right having him here with us. I am fascinated when people end up where they should be. Sadly, there were no parents in his life now. I think I have a chance to be someone special in his life.

A Christmas present dropped into my lap, and no reindeer in sight.

Last night they both arrived from the airport, bags in hand, and went directly to Mike's room.

I saw him in the doorway of the hospital room and instantly fell in love with his kind demeanor and soulful expression. He was unassuming, and willing to walk into a midst of strangers-a family in crisis. But within that family of strangers, was the beautiful woman he had fallen in love with, and he knew his place was with her. He brought to all of us amazing kindness and the ability to induce calm.

They had been in each other's lives for over two years. He was a talented songwriter and musician with an artist's soul. This was our first meeting and without question, he became to be part of the core. He was calm, funny, and incredibly sensitive to our family's state. The loss of his mother to cancer two years before gave him great insight and sensitivity to this family that was heartbroken. And so, here they stood, in a doorway that led to a wonderful man. The meeting of Micah and Mike would be brief, but powerful and important. They were two men who had a mutual love. Jennifer had gone into the hospice room first. I am sure that there is a place in her soul where that moment will remain. She lovingly spoke to her dad of things that were only theirs to share. She whispered something is his ear and smiled. She kissed his cheek; she then walked over and gently guided Micah into the room. She whispered in to his ear. "Dad this is Micah, my boyfriend." Mike's movements were slow and deliberate now, and he didn't do anything unless it had great meaning or significance for him. He raised his right hand slowly to shake Micah's hand and smiled. "Thanks for coming," he said in a slow raspy voice. It made me smile because no matter how much pain he was in, he would find a smile and thanked people for coming. But this time, he seemed to understand the significance of this meeting, as Micah was the man who had won his daughter's heart.

My tears came from my soul as I watched their exchange. Micah reached down and whispered in his ear, "I am so happy that I finally get to meet you sir."

Mike looked into his eyes and waited for more dialogue before he responded. Micah instinctively knew he needed to say more. Because of the recent passing of his mother, Micah understood the moment, and knew the importance of short meaningful exchanges of words when in a hospice room.

He looked at Mike and smiled. "I just want you to know that I'll take care of her as long as she lets me, and that is a promise sir."

He smiled back, squeezed his hand and said. "I know you will."

And he did know. He understood that he was the one. I looked behind me and I saw Kari sitting quietly on the couch. I was unaware that she was there. It was the first time since she arrived that she allowed tears. I looked at her and smiled, to let her know her tears were important. We were all witnesses to a moment in time that was a monumental turning point in the dynamic of a family.

A young man, who spoke softly and simply, but moved me, and said exactly what Mike wanted to hear. They continued their exchange, and a few smiles and kind soft words were uttered.

And in that incredible moment, I felt a wave of anger that made me leave the room, and keep walking. I left the temple and went outside for some air. I could hardly catch my breath I was so angry. I couldn't help but feel that none of it was fair. Micah should have been the recipient of all of his silly jokes, and see the look of pride on his face when his daughter walked into the house. He didn't get to witness how much he loved her, how much he loved us all!

I sat on a bench outside the lobby of the Temple of Doom with my knees under my chin, trying not to get sick. It was then that I started hearing the beautiful piano music. It was coming from the lobby that was adorned in black ebony, green granite, and chandeliers that looked made for a castle. The big brass door swung open, and I saw out of the corner of my eye a gentleman at the piano. He was dressed in a tuxedo, playing a lovely arrangement of *Time in a Bottle* in the grandest of lobbies... the grandest of pianos.

But, the truth is, time cannot be saved in a bottle, and people come in and out of our lives, and our hearts when it is time for them to. The beauty and wonder of our lives is that it always will unfold as it should. I would remember this moment several months later sitting on a boulder overlooking the Lake Superior cliffs. My special moment with an amazing old man who understood that time was never meant to be captured in a bottle, but the magic is in finding a way to capture the memories, your canvas, and to paint them in your heart.

Time… A most profound blessing.

4 DEFERRED DUTIES

The morning cadence was in full swing. The hospice room was quiet and everyone was busy with processing their energy for the day. I was busy spooning ice chips into Mike's parched throat and busy making conversation to try and divert attention from the pain that was enveloping his body. The girls were busy visiting, comforting their dad, and talking to nurses regarding any valuable updates. Kari was sitting on the couch and was busy working the Bat Phone, relaying morning updates to concerned friends on the other end of the line.

Just then, an attractive blond woman walked into the room with a sense of purpose as if she had just been shot out of a cannon, carrying a large file folder. I looked at it curiously as she reached to shake my hand. She sported an important ID badge and a Prada Handbag. Kari noticed the handbag, and her eyebrows lifted, then she mouthed to me, "Who the hell is that?"
I shrugged my shoulders, like how am I supposed to know? She rolled her eyes, smiled at me, and continued her conversation on the phone.

Blondie began to speak and her purpose was unveiled. Drum roll. She was to educate me in the care and cleaning of a colostomy stump, should the decision be made for home hospice care.

Oh no!

My stomach sank, knowing that it was way past a place I could go. It was the moment a bolt popped in my head. I felt the room begin to spin as she talked. All I remember was her beautiful teeth and kind smile, but could barely make out anything else she was saying. I knew her mouth was moving but I didn't have any idea what she was telling me. Something about healing intestinal tissue, proper care for the cleaning an open wound, and blah, blah, blah. The large ominous looking file folder was opened and the "Colostomy Care for Dummies Manual" was revealed, and pushed under my nose like a dish full of dog food! "Blondie with the Important ID Badge" smiled at me, and put a pair of purple latex gloves in my hand as she busily prepared for the procedure. I did not understand what was happening! I looked down at my hand and noticed the gloves, and it finally dawned on me that a "practice session" was about to take place. My knees began to shake as I stepped back and leaned against the wall. I thought to myself, "I can't do this one!" and it made me sad to have to admit it. My eyes began to fill with tears. Kari's instincts quickly understood there was a strange vibe in the room, and ended her phone conversation. She looked between the two of us. She began hearing the one-sided conversation. Her eyes began to bulge out of her head as she saw the "Colostomy Care for Dummies" field kit lay open like a Thanksgiving spread on my husband's dinner tray! She looked at my hands holding the purple gloves and realized what was about to happen...I saw the fire in her eyes...I'd seen that fire before. Just then, a doctor that needed Blondie's attention interrupted our conversation. My dear friend seized the moment. I felt a gentle touch on the back of my elbow and she whispered in my ear, " Enough is enough, now listen carefully, I'll take care of this. You go back to the hotel room and wait for my call." She yanked the purple gloves out of my hand, and threw them in the trash and said, "Go!" I slipped out the door, obeying the command of a woman with fire in her eyes.

As I sat in the quiet hotel room all by myself, I started to find humor in it all and smiled. What was she doing? Did she call the handsome Doctor Vagina? (We could never remember his name, but we knew it started with a V). He was a busy doctor who always made himself available, and of course, Kari had learned the art of paging him.

My grin quickly faded, as I thought about the events of the morning. I could feel tears; tears of regret, fear, and guilt for being unable to do this latest task. "Blondie with the important ID Badge" was a kind and lovely woman, but did not understand. She wasn't aware of what I had already endured out of love in the past year of my life to keep the dignity of a wonderful man in tact. I spent months acting as the "program manager" for his daily care. I learned how to give him injections, organized buckets full of medication, and other "down and dirty" tasks that took me to the brink. Private moments that changed my understanding of unconditional love forever. Blondie had made a grand entrance into a hospice room with a file, a warm smile, and a Prada Handbag, and all she saw was a woman feeding a dying man ice chips. She did not understand the family in the room she was walking into, their history, or their emotional battlefield. That day, my compassion for other human beings became one of the most important lessons of my life. Battlefields; everyone we meet has landed in one during their lives, and carries with them their own scars and wounded hearts. We all have a story. *We all possess a Purple Heart in secret places where no one is allowed.*

As I sat on the bed and waited for the Bat Phone to ring, I listened to an ambulance racing by like a bullet, as it's siren wailed through the streets. I couldn't help but wonder whose family was being tipped over today…who was earning their Purple Hearts.

 The Bat Phone finally rang. "Meet me at the back of the hotel and make it snappy, this is important!"

And then she was gone. "Hey, she hung up on me!" I felt the grin return to my face and giggled. As I approached my destination, I saw a woman on a mission, a trash can, a large pitcher of water, a bottle of warm scotch, two Styrofoam cups hijacked from the Temple of Doom, and one large file folder burning in a small makeshift cauldron!

We toasted to "deferred duties" as we poured warm scotch and shared moments of laughter.

I am not sure why, but I never felt it important to ask her how she slayed the dragon. All I knew was that she somehow became the Blondie Slayer that day, and all that was evil in the moment had been eradicated. And in the end, there were no latex purple gloves worn that day... *only Purple Hearts.*

We laughed, and drank scotch until the file was "ashes to ashes." Laughter. It is a great healer and was enormously important in our lives. A frightening file burning in a makeshift bonfire gave me a feeling of incredible control. The fire in my friend's eyes was extinguished, and the bolt I popped went back into its place. It was another day in the Temple of Doom that brought unpredictable challenges. It was another rollercoaster ride, but it was also another day I landed on my feet, and another day to thank God for giving me armor...I was so happy to have a "Blondie Slayer" in my life.

Laughter...a most profound blessing.

5 MAGIC IN THE WOODS

The fabric in the couch had a beautiful floral print that was soft on my legs. My red dress was pretty and had a Peter Pan collar that made me feel like a princess. My red patent leather shoes had a beautiful ankle strap with sparkles on it. It was all brand new, and if you looked very carefully into them, you could see your reflection. It was one of many occasions that made me think of how great it would be to be all grown up. As I looked at my beautiful shoes, I thought: *Someday, I am going to wear beautiful red high heel "lady shoes" and my feet will hit the ground when I am sitting.*

Later in life, the beautiful red high heel "lady shoes" became an important image for me. It's funny how God implants thoughts and visions in us, even as young children. I thought to myself that some day I'll understand what the big people are talking about and won't feel little and insignificant. But I was happy to be in the joy of the moment, sitting on my Aunt Claire's couch.

Sitting next to me was Jimmy, my brother, who was always there for me and made me happy. He mumbled and groaned about having to wear new clothes. I didn't understand why someone would be mad about wearing new clothes! He itched his leg and complained that new clothes were dumb. Someday his shoes would hit the ground when he sat on beautiful couches too. We would be grown up and doing all the grown up things we ever wanted to do.

We were the middle children. We knew at an early age that wonderful parents loved us unconditionally, but we relished the fact that no one was really paying attention to us… a wonderful realization. The older kids were the "firsts" for everything and the younger kids kept my parent's watchful eye. So Jimmy and I took on the world by ourselves. He took care of me and we had a mutual love and respect for each other that has lasted our whole lives. We would go on long rock hunts in undeveloped land around our house, and sometimes spent hours looking at the clouds and talking about finding gold, but beautiful agates were what we really had our hearts set upon. It is something I like to do more than anything to this day. A wonderful activity, before parents had to worry about bad things happening to small children.

Our back yard had a beautiful wooded area with a stream running through it. He told me it was magical, and it was! It introduced us to tadpoles, frogs, bullheads and sunfish. All of my siblings loved this place, but Jimmy and I spent the most time there. But for today, we were sitting with each other, hanging our feet over the couch and he was telling me a story of a horse named Dora, who lived in magical woods behind our house. If I ever wanted to ride Dora, he would take me there and teach me. He was a six year old with an incredible imagination, and all the wisdom in the world as far as I was concerned. Through the years he taught me so many things. He protected me from harm's way when we played. He kept his promises to me, and when we were much older, he did teach me how to ride a horse in *our magical woods*.

Through the years my brother Jimmy became James. James the attorney, a successful man whose thoughts of Dora and the magical woods were hidden far away in his memory. But not mine. As I saw him enter the hospital room, I desperately wanted to hear more of Dora, the horse that lived by the magical stream, and listen to his stories of where tadpoles came from. His briefcase was full of important papers of finality. I felt so blessed that someone I loved so much could handle such a thing, and I knew he loved me. And as always, he took care of me, and this was the ultimate act of protection. Who knew sitting on a couch with sparkling red shoes and scratchy clothes, listening to the stories of magical places that we would end up here on a very different couch, where our feet hit did hit the floor, and we did indeed understand all the grown up conversations.

James had arrived at the Temple of Doom in a business suit holding a briefcase that contained documents for us to sign. He was a family law attorney who had a passion for those in dire situations and needed help. He came to have both of us sign papers to protect us, our house, our children, but not my heart. The strokes and seizures had taken a debilitating tole on my husband, and he was unable to use his hands. Mike no longer had the strength to read things before he signed them. James lovingly read the documents to him. He worked hard at scratching out an initial signature at least. Mike seemed to understand the importance of what was at hand, and James and I knew that it would take a lot of patience to complete the task. It was an incredible act of will. He fought hard to do this last act of love for me. His frustration flooded my eyes with tears. A man who at one time held a high-powered job in the financial world, fought like an animal to etch an initial onto a piece of paper. An experience that 18 months later, was brought back to me in night terrors and flashback moments, but through the magic of the waters of the North Shore, I was able to leave it on a cliff-side boulder.

And so James sat with me through this ultimate moment of patience and love, and understood the enormity of the act. It was a significant moment as he helped me ride a magical horse of perseverance, to save a man's dignity yet one more time.

And when all was said and done, *he was unable to sign the papers.*

James assured me all would be OK. We walked down the hall, and I saw tears in his eyes. There were no words or stories to make it all better. The innocent world of childhood where beautiful red shoes made you feel like a princess, and magical woods created in your imagination don't translate very well into adult life sometimes. But I held onto the fact that the truest of all magic was in the heart of a brother who loved me, and taught me to trust him and believe that magical places do exist in the hearts of people we love, even when our feet hit the floor.

6 UNDERWEAR

The waiting room was filled with family and friends of loved ones whose lives were broken in half. The hospice waiting room was different than most waiting rooms. There is a constant eerie sense of quiet. There was nothing in our lives but waiting, nonstop waiting. People put together in a room of tables, couches, chairs, and magazines. As I looked into their eyes I saw their wounded hearts. They were a reflection in lives that had all stopped cold, knowing their personal profound changes were imminent. Although few words were spoken, there were occasional glances, and people wondering about each other's story. Fear and heartache is what we shared among us. I found myself bringing coffee, offering hugs and conversation to people who I didn't know, but felt so bonded to. It felt important to reach out and touch their hearts. We were all sharing the same limbo; waiting, in a waiting room full of waiting. *Tick-tock-tick-tock....*

I was so happy to have my core around me: my children, their significant others, and Kari. So many wonderful people had come to be with us. I felt their love every day. The last few days were long and filled with heartache, and we were all were searching for moments of normalcy in the Temple of Doom. This hospital was an extraordinary place with a tempo that beat like a drum. We were surrounded by *the finest of the finest*, all with the same goal. Doctors in white coats would take turns coming and going from patient's bedsides with goals and purpose. But for us, the hustle and bustle of all the heroic care had shifted to waiting and watching, as goals and purpose had faded away. There was nothing to do except wait out the monster, and so we waited. *Tick-tock-tick-tock.*

I sat in a chair looking at a television screen, but not really watching it. It served as a backdrop for a mind whose thoughts were turning to stone. My mind was locked, unforgiving in its vast emptiness. I was comforted by the stillness. The core had graciously relieved me of any social expectations. I was being left alone to breathe in and out.

The previous evening had been filled with emergency messages of horrible turns in the road. My husband's body was fading. The moment was at hand to resign, to sign a document that created finality for it all. His call to heaven would be without a fight now. One stroke of a pen changed the course of my life, a decision that still haunts me. I looked down at my clothes. They encased me, and were a part of the last 48 hours of the most difficult moments. I had slept in them with one eye open, holding the Bat Phone in my hand, waiting for midnight information. And so my clothes and I were a part of a journey that turned to stone, both unchanged in some time.

An emergency "code blue" was announced over the loud speaker. The core did not even blink at the emergency situation, doctors running to save a life that could be saved, but inside his room was quiet. *Tick-tock-tick-tock...*

I looked up at the large table across the room. Five beautiful young men and women whose thoughts were being consumed by a 1000 piece puzzle; laughing, talking to each other, their Bat Phones at their sides, their connection to loved ones and comfort through their day. I watched them banter back and forth, laughing about it all, trying to find the pieces of the puzzle that fit together. Pop, snacks, and magazines cluttered the table, and if you didn't know where they were, you would have thought they were just in somebody's basement. Puzzles, sweet Jesus, puzzles! They were the focus of all attention this week, a good place for thoughts to lie in. They all knew every inch and cranny of the Temple of Doom now. Earlier in the day they went on a mission to heist every puzzle they could find from all of the waiting rooms. They came walking into the waiting room as if they had pulled off the grand heist of the century, real Soprano's mobsters. A nurse caught my eye, and he winked and smiled as he watched the whole thing go down. He was enjoying the show.

Kari sat earnestly at the keyboard messaging loved ones, and connecting with her life, a life that was shifted. When I had called her with the news of Mike's dire situation, she was already out of town for work, living out of a suitcase. She changed her flight as fast as she could and came to be with my family. A suitcase full of dirty clothes was the last thing on her mind.

And so, puzzled children, a wonderful friend, and I were all sitting, waiting. I sat staring at them and my mind could only think certain thoughts right now. Thoughts of this amazing love I saw unfold before me as I sat in my very dirty clothes and head full of enormous sadness. God was sending in the second shift into my life, my core was changing. As they sat bantering back and forth, I thought to myself that they had no idea of the profoundness of the puzzles, the subtle acts of caring and love that I was witnessing, and what it meant for my life. For my children, God was ushering in these the amazing young men, someone to carry on in their dad's place and love them, and keep them safe. Micah looked up at me and smiled; strong and kind, he understood waiting rooms and monsters. The recent loss of his mother and the pain he had experienced, had manifested into a kind and caring demeanor as he understand it all too well. And my baby Babushka doll Heather, found her love in an amazing young man named Craig, who her sister Kimberly nicknamed "Carl". Kimberly always made us laugh, and kept an upbeat energy in the room. He played along with the silliness of his new identity and never questioned it. For being such a young man, he had an old soul, and he knew that he carried an important strength for the puzzled women. Carl was lucky enough to spend time with their father, and share a beer and laughter together. He was the one who understood what their father would have wanted for them in the waiting room full of waiting.

I looked at these fine puzzlers as they bantered back and forth. When there was a quiet moment, I saw them survey the eyes of one another. In those moments, they were nurturing and caring. Walks to the cafeteria, a quiet reflective corner away from the others, where arms were wrapped around broken hearts, and heads landed on shoulders. Puzzle pieces lay still, a reflection of our lives, our fear, and our love for those who were with us in this "room of pending change." No one really understood the change yet, or knew how to do it, and the puzzling became our refuge. *Tick-tock-tick-tock...*

Kari found her puzzle in her computer screen and her phone checking on her mother, who was in her golden years now. A daily phone call at 3:00, inquiring if she had taken her meds, important and loving conversation from a daughter who patiently reminded her of her needs, as her memory wasn't what it used to be. Her mother was such a sweet woman, and tried her best to remember all of things that were important. I sat watching my friend. She was so patient, and yet so humorous about it all. She looked at me with a twinkle in her eye as she rolled them. As she hung up the phone, she looked at me a most perplexed stare. Perplexing enough that I went to her and asked her what was wrong. She smiled and sat back in her chair. "Lamb," Kari said. "I have a problem, I'm out of underwear"

I stared into her eyes as the statement was being processed in my brain. *Underwear*, what? Her puzzled head had turned to underwear!

At that moment for some reason it all became incredibly important. I threw my head back and laughed like I hadn't laughed for what seemed an eternity. The missing puzzle piece that day was clean underwear! Our laughter brought attention from the ever- puzzling table of children. Perplexed grins grew on their faces as they tried to understand us.

Kari threw her arms around me and whispered in my ear. "If I'm out of clean underwear, you know those kids are too." There were no washing machines in sight! She smiled and pulled a pen and piece of paper from the desk. "C'mon," she said, "We need sizes, styles, and color choices! Underwear for Everyone!"

And so off we went, from the waiting in the waiting room. The core stayed back and took it all in stride. TJ Maxx was the North Pole for the day. Shopping carts were filled with gifts from the heart. Games, puzzles, soft clothes, throw blankets and Minnesota shirts for those out of town puzzlers, but most important of all, underwear. God provided an underwear party full of smiles in the middle of a sad and broken place of puzzlers. Pictures were taken of boyfriends modeling the packages of underwear. The other families who were *waiting,* watched the celebration and smiles came to their faces, if for only a moment. Underwear; to make them feel mothered and comforted, when we all needed laughter and a warm moment.

In the evening hours on Easter Sunday, a group of Mennonite singers came to his room to sing. Throughout his stay, they would come and sing hymns, and it was in those moments he would find a smile, and joy filled his face. On this blessed evening, they sang the most beautiful rendition of "Amazing Grace". He smiled, closed his eyes, and slipped into a coma.

Five days later, all the puzzlers were sent home. The monster had played one last nasty card. I could not let them watch the physical changes that were happening while he was in an unconscious state. I needed to protect the Babushka dolls, and save the dignity of the man I loved yet one last time. I could not let them keep that memory warm! I knew in my heart it was what he would have wanted. In the eerie silence heading to the finish, Kari and I remained. The puzzles that were heisted were now returned to their rightful places. In the middle of the night, *the monster had won, and the rollercoaster screeched to a stop...he was gone.*

Tick.

Hospital-care givers were caring only the survivors now, and final documents were signed. A bottle of scotch had been opened, as it was the only way to figure out the next breath, the next move. Belongings were taken and packed painstakingly by

Kari, when I didn't have the bravery to enter that room ever again. The only thing to do was to leave, and puzzles and games from the North Pole were left in the waiting room of waiting, for other puzzlers.

The drive home was interrupted by Bat Phone messages from the organ donor offices and horrible phone conversations were made to people that I loved, that could not even be put on the pendulum of pain. And my mind was like stone again; no words between two good friends, all was quiet. It was done.

Conversation started slowly, as the morning sunrise was about to blossom and erase the saddest of nights. Our conversation turned to buying breakfast foods and even mild attempts at humor. When moments were upon us that felt conversation, Kari would talk me through everything scary, and she grounded me in the fact that I did a good job, although I wasn't sure what that meant. And just when my mind started to fade into stone again, in the quietest moment of the evening, the most beautiful shooting stars streamed across the sky. It ushered in the pending sunrise and the profound changes that had come to our lives. Forever changed.

Forever shifted. And with the brilliance of that symbol, there was a tinge of hope and promise of healing that would start in a car, heading north.

As I listened to the hum of the car taking us home, I thought of the simple things in life that gave me strength. Laughter, nurturing, and the importance of my family who carried me through my pain, and the steadfast love I have for them, who were now in possession of clean underwear. It somehow made everything right in the world, and looking back on the events we had walked through, it all gave me the strength I needed to walk through my darkest days.

Underwear... A most profound blessing.

7 AN EAGLE'S PRESENCE

Two months after his passing, on a beautiful June weekend, I had accepted an invitation to visit my wonderful friends new escape hatch. A beautiful cabin was in the process of being built; arched ceilings and the smell of cedar sawdust were in the air. It was a captivating hideaway in the most exquisite wooded area of northern Minnesota, and was well worth the drive. My good friend Jaana, and her husband Mike were in the process of building a cabin, for the sole purpose of gathering with friends and family to build memories. There was to be fishing and golf weekends, and romantic getaways there. They would surely all happen, *but one would be missing*. It was a quiet and restful sanctuary, with a beautiful wraparound cedar deck that gave view to the most beautiful backdrop of birch trees and starlit nights.

Last fall, plans were being made as two friends engaged in deep conversations over a barbecue pit and a case of beer. Promises were made to finish the work, and thoughts were looking ahead to a wonderful retirement.

I walked into the cabin and was greeted by a good friend who was hip deep in lumber, sawdust, and band saws. He was one of Mike's best friends for many years, and shared the same first name. He was working diligently, pondering the next piece of cedar that would encase the fireplace. All alone in his efforts, it broke my heart.

"Hey toots!" He shouted. "How the hell are ya?" He then took me in his arms and gave me the best of all bear hugs. It was so wonderful to see him. He was a man of few words, but had a soul as deep as the ocean floor, and a heart that was broken.

"Oh my, it's just beautiful, Mikey," I said with tears in my eyes.

"Yep, he said. "I think Doc would have approved." But his look averted my eyes.

My husband was nicknamed "Doc" by his buddies for reasons that were never revealed to me, but it was a name he answered to for the rest of his life.

We exchanged hellos and I felt welcomed at this beautiful new home full of sawdust and love. Sadness felt like shards of glass and underscored pleasant exchanges over the next moments. I knew it would be an important weekend; an opportunity to console a grieving heart. All of us still overcome by the stark nakedness of grief that altered our friendships and our lives forever.

He was quiet, and went to find a piece of cedar for the fireplace.

I heard of a recent trip down to the lakeshore where my husband's friend shook his first at God. In the heat of his exchange with God, a beautiful bald eagle came to rest in a nearby tree. The majestic bird sat there and stared at my friend, as if his presence there was to tell the message. Oh, we should never underestimate God's timing and love! It was a lesson that would repeat itself over and over to me through my journey.

This majestic bird would be named "Doc", a nickname shared with a man who would be forever missed.

My mind recoiled back to Palm Sunday weekend, sitting in a chair lost in overwhelming thoughts, overlooking a window that gave a beautiful view of the Mayo Chapel. Magnificent and symbolic of the strength that I needed to draw upon. Spring had come this week to the world. In its wake, it brought a day of humid air and black clouds that cleared briefly for moments of the sun's rays.

As I looked out the window, I saw rays of sunlight shining down on the chapel's stained glass windows. The sun's rays warming the chapel seemed symbolic of God's comfort. It became an important visual for us all on that day. I was so happy that Jaana was going to be here soon. She had always been there for me, and ignited even a hospice room with her warm smile. I desperately needed her smile today. I wanted her here with him while he was still able to embrace her spirit. The sad news of Mike's imminent call to heaven came early this week and the care he was receiving was quickly turning to compassionate endings. The children were in and out, trying to find their escape valve. I sat with him, and made sure his pain was tolerable and held his hand.

She arrived and walked into the room with the confidence of one who was spiritually centered. Her presence in the room was peaceful, and she understood my terror. The Palliative Care White Coats entered the room soon after she did. For me, it was a fancy name for doctors who specialized in closing the book on patients, and insured their dignity and respect was maintained to the end. They wanted me in a conference to talk about sad the course of events, and sad decisions that were going to be asked of me. I did not want to see them anymore! Amidst these wonderful and valiant efforts, I just wanted to stamp my feet like a child and say *NO!*

Jaana took me out of the room. "Go with them," she said. "I'll stay with Mike, besides, I need time with him alone. You will be fine and they will take care of you, too."

I looked back in the room, and saw them respectfully waiting for me to decompress from their latest request, and found their compassionate gazes directed towards me. My mind was of stone, as I found myself a part of their conference room agenda, and Jaana found her agenda as well.

During my absence, she was able to speak to him of life, love, and the blessings of God. Mike had opened his eyes because it was important. She was a significant vessel to the heavens. She prayed Lord's Prayer with him, and in that instant a lightning bolt cracked, and thunder belched across the sky. The heavens broke open with the most amazing spring thunderstorm. I was in the conference room just down the hall and heard the storm too. I looked out the window and saw a flood of the hardest rain I had ever seen beat down on the beautiful chapel with such strength and purpose. It felt symbolic and cathartic at that moment, as though all of the pain was understood, and the heavens were capable of washing away of our pain and heartache. The doctors who were talking to me stopped cold and looked out the window, too. Papers that needed to be signed lay on the table. They all understood the meaning of this moment. The strength of the thunderstorm was symbolic, and no one's eyes were dry. It was a day of spring-cleaning for the heavens, when all was being washed in preparation for Easter. When I returned to Mike's room, Jaana was sitting in the chair that overlooked the chapel. She got up and hugged me. "Cathy," she said. "He is going to be okay. He saw God." *How does one respond to that moment?* That day, I learned to look at the world that I was left in, to find signs in the simple things like friendship and thunderstorms, and later, an eagle's presence. We are never meant to understand the "why" about moments that feel so divine, but when we find ourselves in them, we are only to find a place for them in our hearts.

The air in the north woods was beginning to chill as the day was ending; as my thoughts were driven back to the cabin I was honored to be a guest at. Its deck was a perfect place to say goodbye to the day. That evening, we all shared a bottle of wine in comfortable chairs staring at the moonlit sky. My friendship with the man who was full of sawdust was new, altered and facing in another direction, which felt good. A necessary change as I felt it was the only way to comfort him. We spent hours talking of important memories, and worked hard through uncomfortable voids in the conversation. He was unaware that I knew the story of the eagle's visit. Later, he shared his story of the eagle, but not much mention of its significance at, except for the fact it was always seen on Sundays. My heart skipped a beat and I could barely breathe with that news, but I did not show my emotions. He was trying to keep himself cloaked, and it felt important not to push him. His ability to share that moment silently was important for both of us.

Work on the cabin continued through the weekend and a rainy Sunday morning. The clouds started to clear around noon, when we all found our way to the deck to feel the sunshine we had been lacking, as the weekend was coming to an end. As if by magical cues from heaven, Doc swooped down through a clearing in the sky, along with three baby eagles and circled the cabin.

Doc has been reported to circle the cabin and since, has only been seen on Sunday afternoons. A beautiful escape hatch in the northern woods of Minnesota, and although someone is missing, his spirit will always live there, in a cabin built from love.

An eagle's presence… A most profound blessing,

8 SNOWFLAKES AND THE SEA

Summer was drawing to an end. It had been six months since his death. I was feeling a call to the ocean; a place I fell in love with. The warm soft breezes were intoxicating, and the power it possessed captured me. There is an undeniable power and strength for those who seek refuge at the sea.

I was trying to get my sea legs back, appropriate for an ocean tale. Legs; when we are born, we spend our infancy preparing them for walking. It is a joyous celebration when a baby takes his first steps. As adults, they move us through the world and they take us places we need to go.

When he died, it was as if I was facing my whole life facing east, and a powerful force had picked me up, and turned me in another direction, forever facing west, forever facing another direction. In the process, I lost my ability to walk, or at least walk without fear.

I was trying to learn to do it all over again. It's when I learned to rely on the people in my life to help carry me. They were the people who picked me up when I needed to walk through the storms without sea legs. There were so many lessons in compassionate love; the loving parents who painstakingly took care of me during the loneliest moments without hesitation. His father Bob, a good and kind man, who did his best to be by my side, and made sure that I had everything I needed. My strong and wonderful sister Mary, who sat with my family as the floodgates of hell opened inside a surgical waiting room. Our lifelong friends, who came and made camp with me, and tried their best to take on the role of a surrogate father for my children, when they needed a father just to sit by them. My youngest brother Tommy, who brought his family down on Easter Sunday, only to return by himself later in the evening, when no one was aware, to just sit with him. My oldest brother Joe, who brought us "good coffee" and homemade scones he had baked. Grandma Helen, who brought her love in a crockpot. Their favorite Pasta Figoli soup was served lovingly, and she refused to let them eat from paper bowls. Beautiful ceramic bowls were bought so that they could feel a sense of home; wonderful gifts of kindness to make us feel loved. My wonderful dad, Poppa John, who wrapped me in the deep strength of his arms and whispered into my ear, into my heart, *"I'll take care of you"*. All the people who stepped up for my children and me, and changed my understanding of human compassion forever. It has all given me a newfound importance and direction in my life; to pay it forward.

One of the most amazing gifts came without fanfare from a wonderful friend, through serendipitous reasons I had reconnected with after Mike's death. We had lost touch through the years, and I felt moved to connect with him again. He was a kind and loving friend who understood my heart, and his compassion became so important in finding my strength and self-worth. He taught me the healing power of light and energy that took its form in mystical snowflakes that I could visualize anytime the pain was too overwhelming. A concept I was a little taken back by. Those beautiful snowflakes saved me from slippery moments, when it was all too much. I learned to love them. I now seek out healing energy every day from snowflakes when I can, as it was the only way my life made any sense. I have learned the importance of sending them back. It's all meant to be shared.

It was time to start walking on my own again. I needed my sea legs back. I knew I had to find the strength. I decided to return to the sea that I loved so much. Writing a letter to Mike somehow made it all a bit more tangible, and I wanted to leave it at the sea. A feeling that I shared with an old frail man with resonating brown eyes, who carried with him a book full of memories that he too captured by writing of them, where he left his thoughts at the waters of Lake Superior for safekeeping.

As hard as I tried, saying goodbye was something that I was unable to do. The ocean with all its energy seemed like an important place to do that. My days were filled with sadness, and I was emotionally barren from the world, as it now existed. It was like looking into a broken mirror. I felt disfigured and distorted, and unrecognizable, even to myself. A frightening dimension of life, and a mirrored glass would never be the same. As hard as I tried, it was forever changed.

I was sitting on the shores of a beautiful California coastline. Jennifer and Kimberly had accompanied me, and Heather kept connected with us on her Bat Phone. They understood and respected the importance of my journey. I was left to do this task on my own, and walked several miles up and down the shore to find the perfect place, nursing a leg that was feeling the pain from a back that needed mending. The September air was cool but it felt good against my skin.

It was the first time that I actually felt him. He was there waiting, I knew he would be.

The shores were filled with people enjoying the beautiful Santa Barbara beach, but I felt alone with him. I found a shell that fit perfectly in my fingers. It was broken, fractured, and disfigured just like I was. But it gave me an amazing sense of energy and bravery for my task at hand. A shell that I carry with me every day; to remind me of snowflakes and energy that helped me through this enormous moment.

And very subtly, without fanfare, I found my moment. I took out the letter that was carefully folded and put in my pocket. "Dear Mike..." and so I read the letter of love to him as the waves crashed into my legs. My tears were cascading down my face and I could barely see the paper I was reading from, but as I finished the letter, I felt his love and smiles. In that moment, I walked into the waters, my shell in one hand, and a wet and wrinkled letter in the other. The words and convictions of the moment needed to go to a magical place where waves would take it away forever. I kissed the letter, closed my eyes, and I felt him. There was a sense of peace to have released it all. It disappeared into the seas for eternity, along with the weight of the world. All that I had left was a beautiful fractured disfigured shell, to remind me of this moment of bravery and change.

As I walked back to my family who were waiting for me, I realized that my life path was changed forever. But I also realized that I could still see the things that mattered most to me. My family; they would always find me in the mirror and never see me as disfigured.

When I returned to them, there was a seaside dinner arranged in a restaurant where we shared laughter and warm moments to celebrate the day. It was all I needed to start my journey back to my life. The monumental moment of releasing him gave me my sea legs back. It gave me my ability to walk the walk.

After dinner, Kim and I found a bench to sit on and take in the evening sea air. It was a wonderful and quiet moment together. We had our leftover food with us, and were finding some conversation that was warm and comforting. A homeless man was sitting near us rummaging through garbage and looking for food. He looked at us with deep kindness in his eyes. His clothes and body were dirty, and told a very different story of heartache; *reminiscent of his battlefield.* Kim turned to him without hesitation and gave him our food. It was symbolic for both of us to know that we could still do good work on this earth, as our new life took hold. Her father had left his mark, his legacy.

As my family and I walked away from the ocean that day, we were all quiet; there were no words spoken, just the sound of footsteps on the pavement. I realized that in my profound day of snowflakes at the sea, my family was getting their sea legs back too.

When I returned home, my brushes and paints were put to work painting the most significant moments on a California shore. It is a painting that I kept in a place so I could see it every day, to remind me of the love Mike had for me, the visit where he was waiting for me. It gave me strength to move through my hardest moments in the days to come, a reminder that my life was going on and I could face my new world. I was facing another direction and the days ahead would be difficult, but I now had the ability to walk through them with strong legs.

So, snowflakes and the sea; strange bedfellows indeed, but I needed the healing power of both of them to sustain me as I said goodbye that day. It gave me the power to look back over my shoulder at the eastern sunrises, and greet confidently the beauty of the western sunsets ... and the ability to love them both.

A sea of change... A most profound blessing.

The Spectacular!

The sea has a way of embracing those

who are standing on its shores.

Breathing in the sea air is like breathing in the universe.

Like the moment of a true love's first kiss,

it awakens the oul,

and suddenly the meaning of life is understood.

The spectacular gift of life! And the way it was intended to feel.

My heart has been drawn to the beat of the waves,

The powerful abyss of the deep rhythmic sounds.

Its mystical aura draws open my mind to knowledge that can

only come from an opened heart, and gently whispers answers in

a language all its own.

God had intended soul searching to be done here.

As I sit alone by its vast beauty, my soul has come in search of a purpose of a broken heart.

A purpose for this life.

I feel the ocean's strength and in turn, I feel it strengthening me.

Slowly, deliberate sounds of the waves caress my soul,

and I weep...

And I heal.

As the sun sets, the salt air chills me.

It is time to move on.

My feet firmly implanted in the moist sand,

I stand and walk away...enlightened

Finding a spiritual presence and a sense of serenity

imprinted in my heart,

Feeling reborn,

Ready for the "spectacular!"

9 PARK BENCH AWAKENINGS

Park benches; I love them. They are made just for people to sit and reflect on, and it's their only purpose and function. They are usually facing something beautiful to look at. And sometimes the benches themselves are home to the beauty of those who sit on them. This bench would reflect one of the most beautiful moments of my life.

It was a good day, and the beachfront park was busy with people delighting in the California sun and enjoying the ocean side view. The warm sun felt cleansing. I came with my sketchpad because it felt like a good day to capture something, but I was unsure exactly what I wanted that to be. Like a rocket, a teenage skateboarder came by me and fell and rolled onto the ground. Ouch!… I used to hate those things, but not anymore. I looked down at him and asked him if he was OK. I saw that his knee was bleeding.

"Oh dang, my mom is going to kill me for ripping my new shorts!" he said.

I fumbled around in my purse and found a Band-Aid and some Kleenex.

I put on my mom hat and smiled.

"Let's at least clean it out so it won't stain them", I smiled.

He looked relieved at the thought of it all. A teenager who I am sure had been at the receiving end of his mother's exasperation more than once. He had a sense of warmth about him, and he seemed to be intrigued with my sketchpad. He had beautiful steel blue eyes that were trying to save face with almost running into me.

"Thank you for helping me; I'm sorry I skated so close to you. I didn't see you sitting there."

I thought to myself, well, his exasperated mom has taught this young man manners and gratitude. But I was secretly wishing that I were speeding down the sidewalk on a Santa Barbara beach too, so I could feel the excitement and freedom.

I smiled. "You're welcome," I said. "I didn't see you either, but you should sit with that Kleenex on your knee for a few minutes so it doesn't start to bleed again, you know, to keep your mom happy."

He looked at me as if he was grateful that I wasn't angry with him. A nice young boy, who was enjoying freedom and speed and was caught in the moment, and now needed to save face with another mom on a bench, with a sketch pad in her lap.

A boy scooped up and dumped into my lap today by the divine shovel. I have learned to stop and listen to it all. He smiled and understood. He was a boy on the verge of adulthood, with the world ahead of him, and the only obstacles in his way right now were an old wrinkled Kleenex, a Band-Aid and a bleeding knee. He seemed comfortable with the idea of waiting for his knee to stop bleeding, and kept looking at my sketchpad out of the corner of his eye. And then he asked me, "Are you a writer or a painter?"

I laughed and said, "I am a dreamer who likes to try both, and you? Do you write or paint?" I realized that he couldn't tell if I had a sketchpad or a tablet.

"Well, I mess around with drawing things sometimes," he said. I sensed a bit of embarrassment in his voice as his eyes looked in a different direction, but I felt he wanted to tell me more.

"Hey, that's pretty cool; it's a nice thing to do sometimes when you need to just chill out."

I wanted to ask him what he liked to draw, but I didn't want to pry into his embarrassed bones right now.

And we sat there for a few more minutes, until he was sure his knee was mended. He was getting up to leave but I saw a hesitation in him.

I said "Hey, now don't kill yourself out there, my dear, but enjoy it! I hate to admit it, but it looks like fun!"

He looked at me and said, "Thank you for not being mad at me; I was dumb", and in the same breath he said, *"I draw hands."*

I stopped cold and understood the importance of the moment. I gave him a few more moments of quiet, in case he needed to say something else, but he didn't. I took my cue.

"Well, that's pretty awesome; hands are difficult to draw, but when done well, they tell amazing stories."

"Well, I don't know why I draw them, it's kind of weird, I just like it".

"Hey," I said, "We don't need to know why we like things, not everything has to have a purpose. Where did you learn to draw, at school?"

He drew a sheepish smile and said, "From this Joe guy, an old dude on the beach. Before my dad died, we would hang out on Saturday afternoons when we could. We used to watch this dude sit and draw people, and I wanted to do it too. My dad got me a sketchpad, and I tried it".

Bingo! It was the reason for getting divinely dumped on a park bench, skinned knee and everything.

"Very cool," I said, and I smiled at him.

Compassion, a lesson I learned from a beautiful blond woman with a Prada handbag, carrying a scary file. This boy was coming from a place with a story that included more than a skinned knee and an exasperated mother. I stopped short for a few seconds, and then I decided to address his comment. "That must have been great to spend time with your dad on the beach. He must have really seen your interest in the old dude's art. I'm glad he got you a sketchpad, to try it out for yourself. Good for you for figuring out how to draw all on your own."

And so we engaged in a nice conversation over the next few minutes. He spoke of the really cool skate park they built on the beach, and all of his friends who liked to go there, and that he had learned a lot of tricks that summer, but his mom was worried he'd get hurt. But what he liked most was to come down and hang with Joe, because he was cool and taught him stuff about drawing.

The tone of his voice became distant, but said confidently; "My dad was Joe's friend before he died. He would meet with my dad and hang out and talk about stuff, too". I looked down by his feet and noticed his skateboard. It had the most beautiful hands drawn on it. It was an image of a boy's hand with a pencil in it, and a grown up hand of a father lay on top of it. A stunning masterpiece; and it took my breath away. I picked up the skateboard and looked at it intently.

"This is just unbelievable, and you have an amazing talent", I said, but didn't look at him right away. I savored the moment just staring at the imagery of a son and his father.

He looked away from me. I would have done the same.

And in that moment, there was a welcome change of thoughts for both of us. An old couple caught my eye as they sat down on another bench that was across from the one we were sitting on. Beautiful old people, whose love for each other resonated in how they looked at each other. We both found ourselves staring at them. I began to feel a sadness come over me and got lost in my grown-up thoughts. Will I ever have that in my life again? How lucky they were to have each other! They held hands and dined on a bag lunch they had packed. They were so caught up in each other, it's as if nothing else mattered. After a few minutes of being spellbound by them, I looked over at the boy who sat just as quietly. I noticed he was looking at them intently, too. He understood, and I noticed he was staring at them holding hands with such intensity.

"Nice hands, huh?" he asked.

"Yes, very nice hands" I said, unable to do anything but continue to stare at them as they were caught in their moment.

I picked up my sketchpad and said,

"Look honey, I know you don't know me, I'm just the lady with a Band-Aid, but I want you to have this sketchpad", and I put it into his lap. "Hands are your connection with your dad. Keep drawing them."

He got tears in his eyes, and said, "I never thought of it like that."

"I know," I said, smiling. I got up from the bench to give him his moment.

"Thank you," he said. *And for the first time he looked into my eyes.*

"You are very welcome. It was a pleasure to share the bench and a Band-aid with you today, my dear."

As I walked away, I thought to myself that everyone, including young boys with lightning fast skateboards, have their own story. It was an awakening in my life that I will never forget.

I have often thought about the sketchpad and the boy. He had found his own personal, profound blessing in an old dude named Joe, who taught him the importance of painting his canvas on a skateboard, and how to keep his memories warm. I will always have etched in my mind the imagery drawn on a lightning fast skateboard, and remember the compassion I felt for a young man with a wounded knee; and a wounded heart. It was the moment that I realized that grief and loss is a powerful journey that takes its shape in many ways. God will always find a way into the hearts of those who have holes in them. And sometimes his tools can be things we don't see coming, like a lightning fast skateboard, and an old dude named Joe.

Encounters you don't see coming…A most profound blessing.

Beautiful Weathered Faces

Tired by the heat of the sun, but comfortable in its presence, they took refuge on a bench.

"Beautiful weathered faces"

Their Hispanic bronze skin was home to years of sundrenched days.

I wondered which one of life's moments was etched into them.

My presence felt voyeuristic,
yet I was unable to stop taking them in.

My heart couldn't let go of the moment.

The years had wrapped their presence around their bodies,

Yet, they looked at each other as if there were no bodies, just those beautiful brown eyes,

There only purpose was to capture each other,
a gateway to their souls.

A place they would visit every time they looked at each other.

They knew that place intimately,

Perhaps never seeing anything else.

I felt my breath get stuck in my throat.

I felt awestruck by the simplicity of their love,

That captured them that captured me.

I couldn't help but wonder;

Did their love start young?

Was there heartache?

Was there joy?

Was theirs a path full of rocks and crevices?

Did their paths ever miss each other?

Did they ever rescue each other?

And I realized in that moment
that none of those thoughts mattered.

They knew to savor the moments now,

And to anticipate tomorrow's joy and hope.

I was witnessing the purest of joy, a true love for the ages,

Quietly, on a park bench.

With no fanfare, no one watching,

Except for me.

They dined slowly, taking in the moments carefully.

Life had taught them this lesson,

And no moment was left to the unimportant.

When the shade had given way to the hot summer sun,

He slowly got up and smiled down at her.

Reaching for her hand,
he stole one more moment to gaze into her soul.

They walked hand in hand on a sidewalk,

Where no one was aware,

No one heard the fanfare,

Except for me, a life changing moment.

10 AWAY IN A MANGER

Christmas Eve. I sat looking out the window as the day was ending, and taking in the beautiful snow that was falling. I couldn't help but be reminded of the significance of snow, whether its form was created in individual snowflakes cascading delicately through the air, or snowstorms. They created moguls in the landscape, they emitted such prisms of white light and for me, and they have become a symbol of love. Each individual snowflake, a creation of brilliance and more exquisite than any lead crystal found at Tiffany's. A wonderful affirmation of God's handiwork! Their splendor has a way of wrapping you in swaddling clothing.

I think it's significant that Jesus was born to us during the snow. Falling snow is like spiritual confetti! It was a comforting symbol of peace for me, and it helped me to walk over the coals that day. I had wrapped myself in swaddling clothes, to move through it all. Christmas Eve *without him;* it had begun.

I looked at the Christmas tree, such a symbol of the happiness and tradition. The tree ushered in the season, and it was always changing through the years. It had been decorated with ornaments made of felt from little children's hands and other handmade treasures. They were all masterpieces in their own right and always put in a place of honor. And in later years, lovely crystal ornaments were given by grown up children, all designed to inspire the spirit in our hearts. But this year, there was no room in our hearts for trees; there was no room in our hearts for Christmas lights, gifting, gatherings, laughter and memories. There was, however, a wonderful place in my heart for my children. They were the ones who had every bit as much disconnect as I did. We all lived in the bubble of fractured reality together. An unspoken truth we all understood.

It was this day that I realized that rituals were changing right before my eyes.

Later that evening, we found ourselves conversing, serving, laughing, and sharing hugs with family. For you see, all who Mike loved were there. Everyone entered the bubble of fractured reality that night with vulnerability and sadness. But it became a warm and safe place. We were all wrapping ourselves in swaddling clothes that evening together, and it was snowing.

A well meaning loved one gifted us with a DVD of Mike's entire life and played it as background to the party, a video collage of pictures, timeless treasures all set to cheesy music. Oh no, a break in the armor! I could see in my children's eyes that it was too much! It was discreetly removed as soon as I was able, for a safer moment.

 Christmas morning: quiet, different. As I opened my eyes and felt morning discover me, I remembered the significance of the eerie silence. A flood of memories of three pigtailed girls waking up at 4:55 in reindeer feet pajamas, sitting like Babushka dolls. Coffee brewing, stockings found, chitter chatter and laughter, fumbling for cameras. But today, silence. My bed felt so warm and comfortable on Christmas morning. A safe refuge and retreat, and I didn't feel sad. I looked out the window and saw the familiarity of the landscape that I fell in love with. Today it was snowing…confetti!

Kimberly had stayed with me that evening. Down the hall I heard stirring and movement in the kitchen. I was trying to hear what she was doing. I sat back and listened, and heard giggles and slamming cupboard doors. Then up the stairs she came. She kicked open my bedroom door. "Hello mother, it's your favorite daughter. And now, my Christmas gift to you! Ta-dah! Breakfast in bed: a bag of Doritos and cheese dip all to go with a cheesy DVD!" *We had found our safer moment.*

She crawled into bed with me and said, "Merry Christmas Mom!" My bed was full of Dorito crumbs and cheese dip and a beautiful soul, who didn't realize it, but she had given me the best Christmas present anyone ever had. Memories were booted up by remote control and we hugged, and listened to a cheesy music. We watched pictures scroll by of a life that once was, a family that once was, before we were encased in the bubble, before we walked through our days, before we had to understand the meaning of the snow, and the importance of swaddling clothes.

We lay there silently, and I knew Christmas morning had ushered in the gift of bravery and the ability to remember the past with a hint of a smile, if only for a moment.

As the confetti fell outside, we were happy to be wrapped in swaddling clothes of our own, lying in our own beautiful manger of Doritos and cheese dip. A most profound moment that changed the meaning of Christmas, forever.

Being brave enough to remember… A Profound Blessing.

11 PROFOUND FRIENDSHIP

The North Carolina morning was cool and muggy. It was a morning of reflection and I had a great feeling of escape, as the trip here was one more level of separation from my life of fractured moments. As I sat in Kari's backyard, I took in her beautiful gardens, which were painstakingly laid out and cared for. It was an oasis for me today. Well thought out designs of foliage, birdhouses and the most exquisite crystals hung in the trees, reflecting both the sun and moonlight, if you paid close attention. Birds were singing, and the North Carolina sun warmed the earth, and began drying up puddles from the midsummer evening rainstorm.

I thought of how good it felt to have quiet peaceful moments by myself. The trip down had been filled with all sorts of wonderful noise and fun. Laughter and deep conversations could change on a dime from being quiet and somber, to laughter and silliness, all meant to find some sense in a world that had gone haywire. Two friends, making the pilgrimage down highways of freedom and escape, a change, if only for a few days. Two friends, whose lives had found each other as young girls, and became harbors of each other's hearts for years, carrying the cross for one another when life called upon them to do so. An incredible journey of friendship that landed us at the Mayo Clinic with a dying man, and profound lessons that changed our lives. It is a gift of friendship that I will always be thankful for, and now, only beginning to understand the significance of it all. It taught me the importance of paying if forward. It's so important in my world that has been full of incredible change; this foundation of friendship never has changed. It was a friendship that acted like a homing device when needed. When the box got tipped over, the other was there to help pick up the pieces, even if they couldn't fix all that may have broken. The task at hand would be to try and pick the pieces up and put them in the box again, even if life was never meant to hold the pieces in the same way. The other would make sure it all at least got into the box again, for safekeeping.

In the last few months, I have felt a movement out of the deep. Mike's passing was a difficult and a harrowing journey, that I am only starting to come to grips with a year later. Feeling the emotions of life that I never thought I could feel; surprising emotions that I did not see coming. Incredibly, through great personal change, I am finding a sense of purpose. It's as if the journey has brought me the strength and wisdom I needed to walk over the coals. My eyes have been opened, and I now see things in others that I hadn't seen before. I learned to understand the importance of other's pain and firestorms. Perhaps it's all given me the ability to recognize tipped over boxes, and when it's happening to a friend...or to make sure their box never gets too close to the edge of the shelf.

In our youth, we were full of great zest and hopeful futures. The thought of tipped over boxes was nowhere in our hearts. She was a daughter of passion, a brilliant dancer by profession, and had a love affair with the arts. She always lived on a golden thread of creativity. A natural sense of design, and an artistic character like no other that was reflective in her soul. A strong and as fiercely independent woman as I have ever seen. She always fought for causes that touched her heart. We both shared a sense for humor, and laughter was center point from the start. It was amazing to hold on to her strings through the years and ride the ride with her, learning so much about independence and freedom of personal expression, wishing secretly that I were capable of the same. Through the years, I always thought as much that as we are alike, we are different; but when my box was tipped over, it was through her that I realized that we were more similar than I ever thought. I realized that my innate need for security and love had come at a high price: *the suppression of my own artistic sense, my ability to be strong and independent.*

Her home reflected her artistic sense. Amazing modern art gathered from all corners of the world encompassed the rooms. When we arrived there, I sat down in a chair weary from the pilgrimage and embracing a most profound moment. I looked at all the art on the walls, and it was if I had never seen it before. I never understood the hue of colors or the artistic vision behind them all. This time they held a vision; compassion, life and meaning. Although I had visited her home often before the box tipped over, I never saw them. That day, they danced off the walls and my heart saw them for the first time. It was a sign of awakening for me. My heart was seeing things clearly and authentically, and I felt such profound happiness that I finally understood that some of the significant changes in my life were good changes. It was the only piece that went back into the box in better shape than it came in.

And as our friendship continues to grow and strengthen, we are still celebrating amazing journeys filled with laughter and happiness. Today, I am finding solace and joy in a friend's beautiful backyard, a place to feel safe and loved, to be reflective in my own ability and new-found strength and of course, to watch closely that her box doesn't go to close to the edge of the shelf. Today I am thankful for her friendship. A Profound Blessing that I am forever grateful for in my life. Kari has taught me independence and strength. As I sat in this beautiful backyard oasis, I realized that she had given me the gift of a lifetime. She taught me that I "always" had the power to pick up my own box when it fell of the shelf, the strength within myself to move through this journey, and most of all, to find my passions in my new life, that would forever be facing another direction.

Friendship... A most profound blessing.

12 A MORNING OF CHANGE

One year later, a year like no other. The sudden winds of change in my life brought me to places I never knew were possible, coals I never thought I could walk over. Today it brought me to this place.

It was a sunny April morning and my back felt the knotted bark of the tree as I sat planting myself up against it. It was a beautiful strong oak tree that had caught my eye on the day we released him into the earth. So beautiful, and it was a symbol of peace for me. It looked so strong and powerful, and at it helped me to move through to that moment of finality. I felt it was important to sit by it again today. The blanket I had wrapped myself in was comforting, warming me against the chill in the air. The cup of coffee in my hand felt warm and soothing.

My insomnia was back, like a stray cat, coming and going when it wanted, when it needed to be fed. My mind had to ride the roller coaster of thoughts out of control again and again, feeding those incessant thoughts of loneliness, fear, and sadness. They were no one's thoughts but mine. I couldn't give them away or put them in a shoebox. So many nights thinking of the journey that unfolded almost one year ago. So many nights staring at the stars through my bedroom window, the ache of the evening with no one to comfort me; wondering what it all meant. I felt like a house of cards ready to collapse.

The sunrise warmed the sky, and made all the engraved granite sparkle like snowflakes. Little mounds of snow were scattered in shadowed places, evidence of the cold hard winter that was changing into warm spring mornings. I could see the sun climbing up into the sky gracing me with picturesque hues of yellow and orange. I thought to myself that sunrises must be God's way of reminding us daily that we are not in charge. *He trumped me again.*

There were so many signs of grief adorning the sparkling granite. Flowers, plastic encased letters, pebbles, and stuffed animals. There were important engraved words and symbols to give dignity and honor; so many names, dates, all in the hopes that aching hearts might make it all tangible.

The breeze ignited the music of wind chimes and the birds that lived among the granite began their daily song, unaware of where they were living. Or were they aware? Huh, another thought. The leaves on the tree that I was making my own today swayed and sang in the smallest of breezes as if it's only purpose was to break the silence. My body and soul tried to find a sense of comfort, fighting hard for it.

My coffee smelled good and I held onto it for dear life, although I don't know why. This place was meant to be a special place for aching hearts. It was meant to be beautiful and peaceful. But for me it was cold, awful, and even though there was a warm sky, everything seemed to be encased in ice. I felt emotionally raped and violated in this place. Finality was gripping me, taking no prisoners; hundreds of granite symbols of cold finality, lined up like soldiers. My knees were shaking through my flannel pajamas, as they always did here. It was an innate response that I didn't understand.

Today was the day that I was going to make peace with this place, make peace with him. I didn't know how I was going to do it, but I felt driven to be here. My existence here was dependent on it. My thoughts drifting back to the day that I read a letter to him at the beautiful shores of the ocean. The ocean was a beautiful place to feel his presence, but not here. But it was important to come here and make peace. I couldn't walk through another day with out finding my heart again. I had lost it. Life in the world was moving on and I was immobile, and I was fighting hard to keep my sea legs.

I was in hands-reach of the soil that encompassed his entity. For what seemed like an eternity of stillness and the inability to move, I reached over and touched the ground, a tangible gesture that I will never forget. For the first time I felt a warm rush of peace go through my body. Tears steamed in my eyes and I cried tears of pain that I pray no one else will ever know, unable to stop, but all the while I felt this warm sense of peace replacing the pain. It was an important moment that was to become another glimmer of change, a chance at finding my heart.

I started to feel empowered and comforted by this feeling of peace. It was strong and it felt right to speak to him. I felt him. I re-wrapped myself in my blanket and sat next to the granite and I began to pour out my anguish. I had to tell him so many things. I told him how proud and brave his children were, and that he was held deeply in their hearts. I told him how much he was missed and loved. I told him that his passions that he did not find here on earth were being ignited in his children, and that they would live their lives honoring him, and that they had learned so much from him, such a good father. Their hearts would go on to find love because of him.

Somewhere during my discussion it happened, I became angry. I was angry with him for abandoning me here. Inner rage, and what I call a *screw you* moment. In a year full of so many uncontrollable emotions, rage had not surfaced until today. I remember being angry, but never being filled with rage. I didn't know rage, never really felt that type of anger, and God ushered anger into my heart like a lightning bolt! I felt God say to me: "Feel this! It's the coals you've needed to walk over to move on. I love you even though you're mad as hell! It's okay to tell the universe to go to hell! I'm still going to be here. I'm still going to make the trees break the silence, make the birds sing you songs, and give you music from the wind chimes. I am still going to gift you with happiness in your life, and yes, I am going to give you a tangible understanding of the past and present and future. And most of all, I am going to help you find your heart; it's as vast as the ocean, and while it's fighting for survival, it's got work to do, people to love, and passions to ignite."

I retreated again under the tree, exhausted, waiting for strength. What just happened? An experience that I shall never quite wrap my head around, but I had full understanding of what was being said to me. He even told me that it's okay to say screw you? I don't remember that in any bible study.

I took another sip of coffee that was now cold; it was all so quiet, but there was a sustained energy now. There was something different. The journey up to this moment in time was grueling; unable to face the duality of the past and present. I couldn't connect the dots! It was if the woman who lived in my body before he died was a different person, and I was just the shell of what was left. I couldn't grab and hold onto the Cathy's hand that had lived in that different world, I couldn't take her with me! She lived behind an invisible wall. She had given birth and mothered my children, loved my husband, lived my life, and yet I could not reach her. That day, in my heated conversation with God, was the day I began to connect the dots and understand the change. It became clear to me that her place was important, as she represented all my memories for me, and she would always "keep them warm". It was the moment I reached out and I held her hand…and felt whole again. She then passed along the baton so "we" could finish the race.

My heart, that was so very broken was healing, a healing that began on a California shoreline. I was beginning to find peace with myself again. I finally felt the ability to embrace the shift in direction, and see the broken shards of glass of my life for what they really were; *beautiful prisms of light.*

I walked away from the icy cold place on a beautiful warm spring morning, with an amazing magical kaleidoscope. I keep it near to my heart to remind me of the importance of the things in my life that have broken me, and through it, the metamorphosis that now was taking place. It seems to me, the only way for the

beautiful prisms to be born; *is if we break the glass.*

Magical kaleidoscopes…a most profound blessing.

13 TIMELESS LESSONS IN LOVE

The chair was warm and comfortable, and felt like home; a chair that had definitely seen better days. Hints of a tear in the fabric, and I thought of how it felt like my life, it was a sign that life had gone on in spite of it all. The chair felt symbolic of how I felt most days, ripped, torn and used up.

Surrounding my chair were mountains of boxes that were painstakingly packed, to insure safekeeping and a sense of order for the change. Encased in my white knuckled grip, I held a piece of canvas my heart painted of a beautiful Santa Barbara coastline that held my sense of hope for the spectacular world that may lay ahead. I needed to look at it every day to remind myself of the healing that was being ushered into my life. I needed it my visual field every time I got scared. I couldn't let this one sit in the truck. It needed to be next to me as I drove away on my journey to the *change*. I needed to strap it in a seat belt and keep it safe.

The boxes were filled with all the memories of what once was. Decisions, so many decisions of what to do with artifacts from the past. Long nights looking through pictures and tangible artifacts, all of which sparked memories. Everything told a story of a family's life, my life that was changing. I felt all of my belongings were being branded with new meaning or discarded, respectfully. I had to make the decisions as to what should be harvested into my new life, to take with me, and what should be let go of with dignity. It was a painful and difficult task, as was with most things in my life these days. But the sorting and harvesting became such a healing tool, a process that helped me make sense of it. I have learned to embrace the positive energy that can be found in pain. I knew pain and positive energy seemed like strange a concoction, but it has been the concoction that's provided me with the most healing.

The moving truck was on its way, and family would be carrying all that was harvested to a new life, a home that was just mine, and Mike would not be a part of it. It would be the place that the people in my life would visit and make memories with just me. Perhaps there would be a gift of grandchildren someday to run and play in my new home. Perhaps others. On the horizon, there was a whole new chapter of memories and beautiful moments that would be mine, and not ours.

Everything in my being was telling me that I was going to be okay, better than okay, and I remembered the beauty of a shooting star that danced across the sky the night he was called to heaven. It gave me such a feeling of peace. It was a moment that I knew would be important in my life. Today is that day. I am feeling shooting stars move through my heart in my sea of boxes, sitting in my torn fabric chair. Awesome!

So here I am, a little fish in a big new pond, anxiously awaiting the truck to take me into a new life. It feels bittersweet, and I am full of anticipation. I didn't know what this moment would bring. I don't know what any moment brings. I feel God sitting in my favorite chair with me, watching it all play out.

God knew the deep chasm of my grief. The people whose laps I was dumped into through my journey had to understand my soul. I'd had to have a deep connection with those who entered my life now, and I would need them all to help me understand it. I knew that they all would be important in my journey. People come in and out of your lives when they are supposed to, a lesson I learned on a sad Thursday afternoon, listening to a rendition of "Time in a Bottle", a most profound, heartfelt circumstance. I learned that a divine shovel drives everyone's life. We end up where we are supposed to be. And so divine shovels, harvested artifacts, and a faith in my *spectacular* someday, brought me to the sea of boxes, the sea of change. I have spent so much time trying to understand my heart... broken, troubled, and ripped apart. And all the while, it was being woven with a golden thread unexpectedly. I never saw it coming or understood it until months later, when a dear kind man, with pockets full of field corn saw it in my eyes.

I walked through my house earlier today. Its stillness was suffocating. It had a different barometric pressure about it now. Walls echoed with the nothingness of it all, but I felt wonderful flashbacks of children in pajamas giggling, angry teenagers working it out in their rooms. Taking in beautiful daughters walking down stairs, and taking our breath away in glittering gowns of almost grownup-ness. All of it seemed to flash through my heart; no family possessions in sight. Freshly cleaned walls, windows, floorboards and floors, as cleaning became an avenue for closure, a desperate cry for my emancipation.

I am not sad anymore; scared, apprehensive, and incredibly anxious of it all; but not sad. It signified the end, the beginning, and my lifelong *heart-work*. The work of a lifetime, and the energy of it all will stay in this house and embrace the new family.

As my thoughts were racing, sitting among the mountain of boxes, I began to think of my sister Mary, the *Queen of Clean* who was my rock in the last couple of weeks. She understood the cleaning I needed to do. To leave this house spic and span. She was armed with a vacuum cleaner, and was cleaning out every nook and cranny in sight. She understood my needs and my physical limitations, as my back was healing from a difficult back surgery earlier that year. The couch was next on her list; to clean the underbelly of it all. Hmm... time to beat her to the punch! I needed to find and clean out what was in there first. The possibilities were endless! My hands felt in between the cushions to quickly wipe away anything that might be embarrassing before she did; socks, readers, chips, maybe all of it. As I was reaching into the deepest cracks and crevices, my hand suddenly found it! It was my sign that life would go on. I had asked for a sign, and my heart skipped a beat as I saw what it was. Tears streamed down my face. A shell! A shell that meant so much, and I had misplaced it. I had spent months looking for it. It was what I held in my hand during a moment in my life that changed me forever. My moment of goodbye on a beautiful ocean on a Santa Barbara shoreline...where a poem was read, and a love was released...and a beautiful *spectacular* was born. The shell had been lost. It had been symbolic and it had my energy in it. I wanted to pay it forward to a dear friend, who let me land in his lap unconditionally. His story now required a shell full of energy, a tangible gift of hope. I put it in my pocket and tears ran down my face. It was a sign that I would be okay.

The truck showed up like a spaceship in my front yard. I had to smile. All was right in the world. My shell was ushered back into my life, and I now had the opportunity to pass it on to someone whose heart needed it just as much as I did. Its imperfection was symbolic. It was just like me! It was the most important piece of tangibility I had ever held. God would help me find my shells from now on if I had faith...happiness would be a part of my life, because I had learned to fall into laps, let God find the good things for me, and help me to understand the power of the timeless lessons of love.

Finding the good things...a most profound blessing.

My Home

It is a place of solitude, joy, reflection, and hope.

A sun filled world that warms my body and soul.

A place for my life to start, to dwell in, and to discover the powers within me...

It welcomes me and I know that

"I am home"

Although my imagination has created it spectacularly,

Its really in my heart, and is where I am, where I allow it to exist

I can take my place of solitude with me to any place I wish,

if I allow it.

It is a wonderful place for creating a reflection of my soul.

My home.

A special gift from the heavens for me to live my life.

Sharing it with those I love,

Is spectacular!

14 A SNOWANGEL'S REBIRTH

It was the second Christmas since Mike's passing, and it was bearing down hard on our lives this year, feeling like a steamroller put on cruise control. Every year, it revs up its engines with carols, Hallmark cards, festive parties, splashings of Santa everywhere, and a sea of blinding Christmas lights.

Today was the day we went to visit the granite soldier, to lay a wreath and do what was *expected*, steamrolling. It was a place that chilled me and made my knees shake, even on warm spring days. The steamroller had landed in the sea of granite soldiers…of course it did. The steamroller's expectation for the day was *"Wreath placement"*. Our family had arrived on a cold morning to the place of finality in a winter that had seen so much snow. Ah, the snowflakes in my life! Looking out of the car window over the sea of granite, the snow was the only thing that was comforting. I got out of the car and stood in it, and I felt it's icy crunch under my feet. A lovely blanket of snow had fallen the night before. I found it ironic that as cold as snow is, it actually insulates us and keeps us warm. One of nature's ironic twists. It was an interesting and prophetic thought for a woman standing in it with shaking knees. I thought to myself as I stared into space trying to hold back the tears, "I wish it would snow". I peered through the trees and saw "his place" back in a quiet corner that nestled up to the woods. I felt myself sigh deeply, rolled my eyes and whispered to myself with a sense of sarcasm, "Just breathe Cathy, just walk through this". No one should ever have to go there, but we all do when the steamroller calls.

A shovel was brought to make a path in the snow, a "yellow brick road" down the path to him! The girls found brave but sad smiles, and engaged in small talk about Christmas shopping. Craig, and Mike's father Bob had accompanied us today to show support, and to leave their heart. Heather smiled at Craig and her grandpa, and she handed a snow shovel to Craig so he could clear a path in the snow down to the granite soldier. He grabbed the shovel and looked down at Kim's silly shoe choice for the day. He rolled his eyes, smiled, and he immediately without hesitation, hoisted her over his shoulder, and off they went. No shovel needed on the yellow brick road for her today! I thought at that moment how my "core" had learned to make the adjustments in their lives too. They all laughed and giggled during the journey down the path, and it became a wonderful icebreaker. As we walked, I looked down the yellow brick road, and I saw the beautiful oak tree I sat under the day I learned to connect the dots. It felt good to look at it again; it was as if it was waiting for me today.

As we stood there next to his marker, the kids bantered back and forth with nervous laughter. They never allowed sadness there and always felt their dad's quick wit and personality should be honored in this place. It was what he would have wanted. So, in another ironic twist, the place incased in ice and sadness for me became a warm place of laughter and smiles, as if Mike were standing among us. I knew that their father would have understood this reaction to it all; and he would have done the same. And then the moment came, as smiling faces became still. "Wreath placement"... steamrolling.

They all watched quietly as their grandpa secured it in the frozen ground, to stake a claim on it. I could not watch. I looked up and tried to swallow up my sadness as to not break the mood for my children. And through the next few moments, they all hugged each other. Kim finally broke the sad and somber moment and said " Ho Ho Ho Dad!" and they all laughed. Looking back on it, it was very funny. I however, did not laugh in that moment, I did not talk, my knees shook and my eyes steamed up. I was counting the minutes before I could walk away without anyone noticing my hatred for the moment. I prayed for strength. And then, it happened.

The most beautiful snowflakes started to fall to the earth! The biggest snowflakes any of us had ever seen! Conversations stopped cold, and everyone looked up to the heavens and watched the loveliest ballet of snow! It was brilliantly choreographed as it fell to the ground. It was as if the sparkling little pieces of magic all knew exactly where they were to land, symbolic of a family fighting hard to find their place to land in the world too.

Snowflakes, my heart needed them today, and in the moment when I was full of anger and sadness, they had fallen and emitted such an energy, warmth, and peace. Although I had spent months visualizing them in my head, here they were, *tangible;* big, bold, beautiful, and making a stunning landing as they fell from the sky!

Heather said, "Mom, look at those things! they are huge!" as she tried to grab them out of the air. She looked curiously at me and smiled, "Do you think it's Dad"? I sighed again, this time a sigh of happiness, and said, "Of course it is".

The beautiful landscape brought back memories of the Babushka dolls in snowsuits, playing outside with their dad during a storm that brought record-breaking snow. That morning, a huge slide was constructed off the back of the garage. A loving dad had created it, so they could feel the freedom of movement and the fresh air that only comes after a new snow. It was in another time, another world, when small children delighted in sliding down a wonderful hand made slide built by their dad, and snowmen, snow angels, and most importantly, wonderful memories were born. A reminder to us all, of the priceless gift of "creating memories" for those we love in the world. Keeping memories warm, even on a cold and snowy morning. The grandeur of this wonderful slide eventually melted, but it's memory lives warmly in the hearts of grown up children.

As the wreath glistened in the cold winter sun, in our new world, we all took in the moment. They all laid down in the snow, silly shoes and all, and watched the ballet together. They needed to lie down by their dad, and they reminisced of the wonderment of the snow slide. And in the midst of the moment, arms and legs started to move, and the most magnificent snow angels were "reborn".

I realized on that day *we would all learn how to land. Because just like the snow, we are predestined to land where we are supposed to land.* And when we don't know what to do, we will be carried, and no shovels will be needed. I finally understood the peace of this place, and in turn, I had made peace with "it". And on that cold and snowy morning, the steamroller was stopped cold, and there were no longer expectations in this journey of wounded hearts. A steamroller stopped cold.... A most profound blessing.

15 INCANDESCENT STRENGTH

The candle was burning on the table, as if it had a purpose and a life all its own. A beautiful blue candle that smelled like fresh air and its aroma was how love would feel if you could smell it. It was a candle that sat with confidence on my table. I don't find comfort in many things these days, but I happened to find a warm friend in its flame. A silly thought maybe, I really don't know. I am comforted by its dancing light on the days when I can't find a safe place to land, on the days nothing makes sense.

A wonderful therapist, who I sought out when my life became too slippery, asked me to do three things. My task at hand for the last two months was to find a candle, buy a book on the *monster*, and find a place to read and reflect. One, two, three strikes, you're out! I was unable to accomplish such simple tasks. It was all too close to the pain. I tried hard everyday to do what was asked of me. I went to stores that were full of candles. There were so many to choose from. But buying one to represent his presence in my home, my heart? It seemed so simple, but no, no, no! Too scary; it was pressing the balloon way too hard. *Strike one!*

I was to find a place to grieve. My home was beautiful to me; shades of warm color and large windows that created sun-drenched afternoons. I felt comfortable in every room, but I could not find a place safe enough to be reflective and provoke thoughts on his death. It too seemed so simple, but no, no, no! Too scary; it was pressing the balloon way too hard. *Strike two!*

I was to find a book on grief to read. I was given all kinds of books on love, loss, and finding my way back; stacks of them. The pages filled with metaphors, clichés, sadness, spiritual journeys and scripture. My mind did not let me read them yet. The moat around the castle was full of sharks. Reading a well-written book about the monster would bring it all too close to the surface. You'd think I could have just picked one out of the pile, perhaps I could write my own book. But no, no, no! Too scary; it was pressing the balloon way too hard. *Strike three!* Damn.

So what does happen when balloon gets pressed too hard? It bursts and everything inside of the balloon escapes. Pure escapism. We all need to escape sometimes, and perhaps the pain and fear that lives in the proverbial balloon just wants to escape. I eventually realized that my tasks at hand were designed not to burst the balloon, but to let the air out slowly.

And then one day a friend gave me a candle. It was a candle with brilliant hues of blue. It was a lovely gesture from a friend, but she was unaware of the profound meaning it had for me. It was a simple act of thanks for a recent evening together. The candle was a gift of kindness and friendship that she left on my doorstep while I was away, and it moved mountains for me.

I now have my candle. It burns for me every day and keeps the monster at bay. It was such a lovely gesture of friendship; I knew it was the one. It lights the tarmac for me when I am searching for my safe place to land. It whispers important thoughts to me if I listen closely enough. And most importantly, it effortlessly, without fanfare, has let the air out of the balloon slowly and safely, just enough for me to trust it.

So God made sure this landed in my lap. It must have been important. Everything that is scooped up in that divine shovel is significant. The candle is a constant reminder of the love I have for my friend, all my friends, and people in my life, who lift me up and keep the candles lit; *and never let me strike out.*

Candlelight… A Profound Blessing.

16 SCARS

Scars. We all are branded with them, and they are a reminder to the world that we have had trauma and pain. A reminder of a brand new red tricycle that met the force of a sidewalk pavement, or a home run ball that raced faster than a baseball cleat skidding into home base. The world is full of harmful things... scratching us, hurting us, and marking us.

Our bodies are not meant to be open to the things that destroy or hurt us, or our souls. Scars are the most magnificent of miracles. It is a sign that God is working overtime. Spectacular new skin is created. It is a concoction specially made, to protect and shield us where we have been hurt, and are the most vulnerable. A stronger skin with superpowers to keep guard, protect us in our most vulnerable places, where we have been hurt the most. A visual reminder of change, through love.

The Scars of the heart. Unseen to the naked eye; but if you look closely enough, you can see them in the deepest chasms of people's eyes. It is a sad and unforgiving place. I am glad we live in a world of scars. It's as if we are branded with a stamp, to be a constant reminder of deep love that God has for us, and that He will always be there to mend a wounded heart.

As I travel through this grief process, I have come to understand the importance of good scar tissue. Although it leaves me altered, different, feeling ugly at times, I keep close to my heart the notion that I can be healed, not by myself, or by others, but through the strong healing powers of the God ...if I let him

I will wear my scars as a beautiful crown, because now I understand their significance to my survival. And when I look at them, they remind me that I am stronger, braver, and being reinvented every day through the grace of God.

Scars... a most profound blessing.

17 STEP OUT OF THE BOX AND DANCE

Excerpts of a letter from a great friend:

Dear Leafer,

You've been through it all. It's time for you. Time for you to start living again, smiling again. C'mon girl "buck up!" Take all you have learned and imprint it within you. Put all the sadness on a shelf somewhere. And on those days that you find the shelf, put on those red high heels you are always talking about, and step out of the box and dance! Your life is waiting for you! Flush the black veil or trade it in for something else black and Lacy. Ha-ha-ha...

A most profound letter ... gulp.

There they were: the most fierce red stiletto heels, sitting on a shelf at Bloomingdales, staring me in the face. I wanted them. They were the key to my emancipation. So crazy, I know. Red shoes. It was coming from a wonderful memory from my childhood. When a little girl sat on a couch wearing the most beautiful sparkly strapped red shoes, and dreamed of being all grown up and wearing the lady version of red shoes someday. The first steps to happiness should be taken in a killer red stiletto shoe. Red is the color of power and strength. I want to be powerful and strong. My sea legs are ready to dance in them, or to at least walk across the floor in them, anyway. It would be well worth the price tag to just walk across the dance floor in them.

As I stood in the store staring at the red lady shoes, I thought about my days as a young girl taking dance class in a basement that was converted into a studio. There was an elegant portrait of an exquisite dancer in a blue tutu and tap shoes that hung on the wall. She was a woman who found her passion in teaching dance. Putting on tap shoes, or holding onto to a ballet barre, I always felt so happy and powerful there. Looking into the large mirrored wall made me feel free, strong, and I never saw myself as disfigured in it. As I think of my dance floor, my heart turns to the recent passing my mentor and the dance teacher in my life. When I think of her, I have a vision of her standing at the back of class, watching us with the most intent brown eyes. She understood her students, and knew their abilities, and their hearts. She was a woman of few words, but if a glancing nod came my way, I was on top of the world and knew I had done well. Shirley Larkin, a legend in her profession, who always taught us to "dance as if it were our last step!" I will Mrs. Larkin, I feel your glancing nod, and I will think of you with each and every step.

And so the story of profound blessings of my life has unfolded. My sea legs are getting strong and the western skies are becoming more beautiful every day.

A journey of change, a journey that has brought me to a new awareness on this planet that I got left behind on. I am a woman who now finds gratitude every day for the rocky path I have walked. I've learned to take care of what's left of me, and not let the monster anywhere near me or the dance floor! Although I am far from being over the rainbow, I see it in plain sight. In moments when I have felt the most alone, I have been given blessings to weather the storm. I have finally become aware that some days, I can wake up and realize that God has replaced some of the sadness with a happy thought and a smile.

On an extraordinary day, I was lucky enough to befriend an amazing man who walked up a steep hill, to step out of his box and dance on a Lake Superior cliff. A man who understood that love never leaves you, but it can change, and golden threads can be weaving themselves into your path, although you may not be aware of it. He was a remarkable man, although frail, old, and walked a cane, had a beautiful heart that kept his life worth living. But most of all, a man who gave me my chance for emancipation, as he taught me to save my memories, and keep them warm.

It was a difficult and very intimate path to write of this journey. And as it unfolded, I felt a cathartic movement in my heart. My hope in telling this story is that it could somehow validate another person's brokenhearted journey of monsters, steep cliffs, and change in direction. During profound and life defining moments, finding strength in our lives may seem like an insurmountable task, but if you look hard, and are "still" and listen for it... it will always find its way to you.

And so I have found my red shoes. I wear them with grace and dignity, with a sense of freedom and power, for they represent my new found-strength. And as I move across the dance floor in my red shoes, I will never forget the journey that took me up the hillside to where my heart ran free. I finally conquered the cliffs that made me brave and strong enough to dance again...in the most amazing "red lady shoes."

There will always be a dance floor when we are ready to dance!

Perhaps the most profound blessing of all…

"PROFOUND BLESSINGS"

Discussion Guide

In the first chapter of the book, the author makes a visit to the North Shore of Lake Superior to let her heart "run free". What do you think she meant by letting her heart "run free?"

Where would you go, or what would you do if you needed to let your heart run free?

The author speaks of her serendipitous encounter with an old man who changed the course of her life. Serendipity, fate, and destiny...discuss any serendipitous moments you may have had in your life?

What are your little "black book" memories....God's golden threads?

There are several references made to unconditional friendship. When her husband passed, she could not go back into his room, and her friend took on the task for her. Would you have been able to do the same?

Describe a time when you have had to rely on a close friend to be a "Keeper of the Keys"?

Describe a time when you have been able to help a close friend.

"Compassion…everyone has their story, their *emotional battlefields"*, where no one is aware. What do you think the author meant by that?

What do you think the significance of clean underwear was in this story? Why did it provoke a shopping trip, and smiles and laughter in a sad and scary place?

Laughter became very important, during an extremely sad time. Moments of laughter can shoe up when it is least expected sometimes. Can you think of a moment when you found laughter in difficult circumstances?

Red shoes reflected memories for the author as a young child. For her, they were a symbol of strength and bravery. What experiences, relationships, or things made you feel brave and strong in your childhood?

During difficult times, people often have to make hard decisions. In the final days of her husband's life, his physical appearance became distorted, and she made the tough decision to send her children home before his death. She felt it would have been his wish.   What would you have done if it were you in the situation?

In the middle of the cemetery, she describes her feelings of grief as the inability to find herself. She said she couldn't connect the dots... What did she mean by "connecting the dots?"

One of the most important lessons in the story was the concept of keeping memories "warm". How do you do keep your personal memories warm with those you love? Discuss what you might do differently after reading the book

At the end of each Chapter the author identifies a profound blessing. Every moment in one's life has a defining profound blessing. What are yours?

What did the author mean by "There will always be a dance floor when you are ready to dance"?

In loving memory of

Michael B. Leaf

A man who understood the importance of life's journey,
lies in the passions that are found along the way

Catherine Capra-Leaf is a life long resident of Minnesota. She graduated from Mariner High school in White Bear Lake in 1976, and attended the University of Minnesota: Duluth. She was married in 1979 to Michael Leaf, and has three daughters, Jennifer, Kimberly, and Heather. She has worked in the White Bear Lake Public Schools as a paraprofessional for 21 years, working with special education students. In her spare time, she enjoys painting, walking, being with family and friends, and her new found love of writing.

Helping others who are walking through their own difficult journey to find their strength is the main focus of her life now. She continues to write stories to inspire and encourage people to find healing in their own lives.

Photographer: Erin Harder Zealley

Make up Artist: Dakota Kuhn

Cover layout and design: Jennifer Leaf

Made in the USA
Charleston, SC
09 September 2012